The best of Mrs BEETON'S Jams, Pickles & Preserves

The best of Mrs BEETON'S Jams, Pickles & Preserves

WEIDENFELD & NICOLSON

First published in 2007 by the Orion Publishing Group Ltd
5 Upper St Martin's Lane
London
WC2H 9EA

Designed by seagulls and cbdesign
Index prepared by Chris Bell
Produced by Omnipress Ltd, Eastbourne
Printed and bound in the UK by
CPI Mackays, Chatham ME5 8TD

Contents

The Art of Preserving

*Rows of glistening home-made preserves with
excellent flavours are ample reward
for the simple methods and
equipment required.*

ACHIEVING A SET

Three ingredients are essential for a good set – pectin, sugar and acid. When these are correctly balanced the mixture will set.

Pectin
Naturally present in some fruit, this is the glue-like ingredient found in cell walls. It is extracted by cooking, assisted by the presence of acid.

Sugar
Sugar is added in proportion, depending on the pectin content of the fruit, then boiled down to the right concentration for producing a set.

Acid
Some fruits contain enough acid; some with a low acid content require the addition of lemon juice for making a good preserve. Not only does this promote pectin extraction but it also helps to give the preserve a good colour and sparkle.

INGREDIENTS

Fruit
Fruit contains the maximum amount of pectin before it ripens; however, in this state its flavour is not at its best. For a good preserve, the ideal is to use some fruit which is not quite ripe along with ripe fruit for flavour. Overripe fruit is not suitable for set preserves, although it may be used for fruit butters and cheeses.

It is important to know or to check the pectin content of the fruit. Refer to page 10 for a guide to the pectin content of some common fruits. Fruits with a low pectin content may be combined with others which have a high pectin content, thus ensuring that the preserve sets well.

Acid
If the fruit does not have a good acid content, then this should be added in the form of lemon juice. It should be added in the initial stages of cooking to assist in pectin extraction.

Sugar
Sugar should be measured carefully: too much will cause the jam to be syrupy, not set; too little and the jam will require long boiling to give a set at all, making it dark and overcooked.

Any sugar can be used. However, special preserving sugar gives the best results as the large crystals dissolve slowly and evenly, producing less scum and giving a sparkling preserve. This said, granulated sugar is probably the more frequently used type and it is perfectly acceptable.

The practice of warming the sugar before adding it to the cooked fruit helps to make it dissolve evenly and quickly.

Special sugar with pectin and acid added in the correct proportions for setting should be used according to the manufacturer's instructions. The boiling time is usually significantly shorter than with traditional ingredients. This type of sugar is very useful with low-pectin fruits or with exotic fruits.

Pectin

Bottled pectin is also available for use with fruits that do not contain a good natural supply. Again, this should be used exactly according to the manufacturer's instructions.

Alternatively, fruit with a good pectin content such as apples, redcurrants and gooseberries may be cooked to a purée and used to set preserves that do not contain sufficient pectin. The purée is known as pectin stock. The whole, washed fruit (trimmed of bad parts, stalks and leaves) should be cooked to a pulp with water, then strained through muslin. Pectin stock may be combined with fruit such as strawberries, cherries or rhubarb to make a set preserve.

EQUIPMENT

Cooking Pan

Do not use aluminium, copper, uncoated iron or zinc pans as these bare metals react with the fruit, adding unwanted deposits to the preserve and in some cases spoiling both colour and flavour.

A stainless steel pan is best. Alternatively, a heavy, well-coated (unchipped) enamel pan may be used. Good-quality non-stick pans are also suitable.

Although a covered pan is used for long cooking of fruit that needs tenderizing (especially citrus fruit for marmalade), for boiling with sugar a wide, open pan is best. The wider the pan, the larger the surface area of preserve and the more efficient will be the process of evaporating unwanted liquid to achieve a set. Whatever the shape of pan, it is essential that it is large enough to hold both cooked fruit and sugar without being more than half to two-thirds full, so that the preserve does not boil over when it is brought to a full, rolling boil.

Knife
Use a stainless steel knife for cutting fruit. A carbon steel implement reacts with the fruit causing discolouration.

Sugar Thermometer
This is invaluable for checking the temperature of the preserve.

Saucer
For testing the set.

Jelly Bag and Stand
For making jellies and jelly marmalades you need a jelly bag and stand to strain the cooked fruit. You also need a large bowl to collect the juice. If you do not have a stand you can improvise by tying the four corners of the jelly bag to the legs of an upturned traditional kitchen stool by means of elastic. Instead of a jelly bag a large, double-thick piece of muslin may be used.

Jars
Use sturdy, heatproof jars that are thoroughly cleaned, rinsed in hot water and dried. Unless they are exceedingly dirty or have food deposits, there is no need to sterilize jars. However, they must be washed in very hot soapy water (use rubber gloves to withstand the heat), the rinsed in hot or boiling water. Turn the jars upside down on folded clean tea-towels placed on a baking sheet or in a roasting tin, then put in a warm oven about 15 minutes before use.

Alternatively, wash the jars in a dishwasher just before use and leave them undisturbed to avoid contamination. They will be hot and perfectly clean.

MRS BEETON'S TIP

If you make a lot of jam, it is worth investing in a good quality preserving pan. Stainless steel pans are best. Avoid iron, zinc, copper and brass pans as the fruit will react with the metal. Cooking in copper can enhance the colour of jams such as green gooseberry but the use of such pans is no longer recommended.

Jam Funnel
A wide metal funnel which fits into jars and makes filling them far easier.

Small Jug
For ladling the preserve into jars.

Covers and Lids
The surface of the preserve should be covered with discs or waxed paper. Airtight lids should be plastic coated as bare metal will react with fruit acids in the jam and corrode. Cellophane discs may be used with elastic bands; they are not ideal for long-term storage but are useful under lids which may not be well-coated with plastic.

Labels
It is important to label each pot with the type of preserve and date.

PREPARATION TECHNIQUES

All fruit should be trimmed of bad parts, stalks and leaves. Then it should be prepared according to type – peeled, cored, stoned, cut up and so on. All these trimmings including any pips, should be tied in a piece of scalded muslin and cooked with the fruit, as they contain valuable pectin.

Make sure you have enough clean and warm jars, covers and labels.

COOKING TECHNIQUES

Cooking the Fruit
The prepared fruit should be cooked with acid and a little water if necessary. Soft fruits and others that yield a good volume of juice need only a little water to prevent them from drying out in the first stages of heating. The fruit must be initially cooked until it is thoroughly softened, preferably in a covered pan to prevent excessive evaporation. It is at this stage that the pectin is extracted. Undercooking not only results in tough pieces of fruit in the preserve but also in insufficient pectin for a good set.

Adding Sugar

When the fruit is thoroughly cooked the sugar may be added. If possible warm the sugar first, then add it to the fruit. Keep the heat low and stir until the sugar has dissolved completely. This is important – if the preserve boils before all the sugar has dissolved, this may encourage the sugar to crystallize.

Boiling until Set

Once the sugar has dissolved, the preserve should be brought to a full, or rolling, boil. This rapid boiling concentrates the sugar to the level needed to balance with the pectin.

Skimming

At the end of cooking any scum which has collected on the surface of the preserve should be removed with a metal spoon. Sometimes a small knob of butter is added to disperse this scum or any remaining scum which cannot be removed.

Removing Stones

If fruit is not stoned before cooking, the stones may be removed with a slotted spoon or small sieve as the preserve boils.

TESTING FOR SETTING

It is important to turn off the heat off or take the pan off the heat when testing for setting. If the preserve continues to cook it may boil beyond the setting point, then it will not set.

Flake Test

The least reliable. Lift a mixing spoon out of the preserve and allow the mixture to drip off it. When setting point is reached the preserve does not drop off cleanly but it tends to fall off, leaving small drips of flakes building up on the edge off the spoon.

Saucer Test

A reliable method: have a cold saucer ready in the refrigerator, spoon a little preserve on it and set it aside in a cool place for a few minutes. Push the sample of preserve with your finger; it should have formed a distinct skin which wrinkles. If the sample does not have a skin, the preserve will not set.

Temperature Test

The best test: when the correct sugar concentration is reached the boiling preserve should achieve a temperature of 105°C / 220°F. Do not let the temperature go any higher.

POTTING

Before potting, warm the jars and spread clean tea-towels or paper on the surface where the jars will stand. Have ready a tea-towel to hold or steady the jars (an oven-glove is too bulky) and a dry tea-towel or absorbent kitchen paper for wiping up any bad spills on the jars. Never wipe the jars with a damp cloth or they will crack.

Most preserves should be put into jars as soon as they are cooked. The jars should be full but not overfilled. There should be just a small space below the rim of the jar to prevent the preserve from touching the lid. Cover the surface of the hot preserve immediately with a disc of waxed paper, wax-side down, the put the lids on at once.

Preserves with pieces of fruit or rind which tend to float should be left to stand for 15 minutes after cooking and before potting. This allows the preserve to set just enough to hold the fruit or rind in position. The preserve should be stirred and potted, covered with waxed discs, then left to cool completely before covering with lids.

STORING

Store preserves in a cool, dark cupboard. They will keep from 6–12 months or longer in the right conditions. Since most modern homes have central heating, preserves tend to dry out during storage by slow evaporation. This can be averted if the rims of lids are sealed with heavy freezer tape.

PECTIN CONTENT

To make a fruit jam you should know the pectin content. Fruits with a good pectin content require an equal weight of sugar. Fruit with an excellent pectin content – currants, gooseberries or apples – can take up to 1.25kg / 1¼ times their weight in sugar. Fruit with medium or poor pectin content will only set 0.75 / ¾ their weight in sugar. See page 10 for a general guide to pectin content. If the pectin content is poor, add pectin stock (page 3), plenty of lemon juice or commercial pectin.

DEGREES OF SUGAR

It is easier and much safer to use a saccharometer (a sugar thermometer) than to test the syrup with your fingers. If you really must use your fingers, dip them in iced water before lightly touching a small sample of the solution in a saucer. **NEVER** dip fingers into bubbling syrup.

PECTIN TEST

*Place a little methylated spirits in a clean, old jar.
Add a spoonful of the thoroughly cooked fruit pulp
(before sugar is added) and gently swirl the mixture.
Allow the pulp to settle. If it forms a large lump,
the fruit has a good pectin content. If there are a few
lumps, then the fruit has a moderate pectin content.
If the pulp is separated in lots of small lumps, it has
little pectin and more should be added for a good set.
These lumps are known as clots. Discard the jar
and its contents after testing.*

Small Thread (102°C / 215°F) – when a short, fine thread is formed when the forefinger is dipped into the solution, touched to the thumb and drawn apart.

Large Thread (103°C / 217°F) – when a longer thread is formed.

Small Pearl (104°C / 220°F) – when a longer, thicker thread is formed.

Large Pearl (105°C / 222°F) – when thumb and finger may be stretched as far as possible without breaking the thread.

Small Blow (110°C / 230°F) – when a little of the solution is scooped into a perforated skimming spoon and bubbles are formed when air is blown through the holes in the spoon.

Large Blow or Feathers (111°C / 233°F) – when more bubbles are formed and fly off the spoon like feathers.

Small Ball (114°C / 237°F) – when a small drop of sugar solution hardens in cold water to form a small ball.

Large Ball (119°C / 247°F) – when a larger ball is formed.

Small or Soft Crack (143°C / 290°F) – when the sugar partially sets and sticks to the teeth when bitten.

Large or Hard Crack (155°C / 312°F) – when a drop sets hard and brittle in cold water.

STRAINING FOR JELLY

When making jelly great care must be taken that the syrup and fruit juice is not boiled too much, otherwise the colour will be entirely spoiled and the liquid will become thick and ropy like treacle. When the syrup and fruit juice has been sufficiently boiled it must be passed through a fine sieve or a jelly bag to clear. An excellent substitute for sieve or jelly bag, if these are not available, may be improvised by turning a chair upside down and tying a clean piece of coarse linen or muslin to the legs of the chair. Place a large bowl underneath and pour a basin of boiling water through the linen. Remove the bowl directly the water has run through the linen and substitute a clean basin, then pour the liquid to be strained gently through the strainer. Repeat this process two or three times, if necessary, until the jelly is perfectly clear. The liquid should not be interfered with or it will be rendered cloudy. Always scald a jelly bag before using it.

Fruits such as apples, gooseberries, quinces, Seville oranges, redcurrants and those containing a large amount of pectin are most suitable for making jelly.

THE PECTIN CONTENT OF FRUITS

Note that pectin content tends to be highest when fruits are most acidic, so that the pectin content of any particular fruit may change depending on its ripeness. It is a good idea to use the Pectin Test on page 8 to ensure good results.

High Pectin
Citrus fruits – oranges, tangerines, lemons, limes
Crab apples
Cranberries
Currants
Gooseberries
Lemons
Most plums
Quinces
Tart cooking apples

Medium Pectin
Cherries
Elderberries
Grapefruit
Most grapes
Melons

Rhubarb
Ripe blackberries
Sweet apples

Very Low Pectin
Apricots
Blackberries
Blueberries
Figs
Guava
Nectarines
Papaya
Peaches
Pears
Pineapple
Pomegranates
Raspberries
Strawberries

Jams & Preserves

Utilise surplus and seasonal produce and transform it into delicious, natural preserves. For perfect results, accurate measuring is essential.

APPLE JAM I

**To each 450g / 1lb apples, weighed after being pared,
cored and sliced, allow 350g / 12oz preserving sugar,
finely-grated rind of 1 lemon and juice of ½ a lemon**

Choose firm, sound apples of the same kind; peel, core, and cut them into thick slices. Barely cover the bottom of a large preserving-pan with cold water, add a good layer of sliced apples, cover thickly with sugar, and sprinkle with lemon rind and lemon juice. Repeat until all the materials are used, cover the pan and stew gently until it may at once be put into the pots.

APPLE JAM II

**1.8kg / 4lb sour apples
1.4kg / 3lb preserving sugar
finely-grated rind and juice of 2 lemons
2.5 ml / ½ tsp ground cinnamon
150ml / ¼ pint cold water**

Pare, core and cut the apples into thick slices. Place them in a preserving-pan, add the sugar, lemon rind and juice, cinnamon and water, and cook gently until reduced to a pulp. During the first part of the process stir occasionally, but towards the end, when the greater part of the moisture has evaporated, stir more frequently to prevent the preparation sticking to the bottom of the pan. Pour into jars, cover closely, and store in a cool, dry place.

APPLE AND BLACKBERRY JAM

900g / 2lb blackberries
2kg / 4½ lb preserving sugar
1.8kg / 4lb apples

Pick the blackberries, put them into a preserving-pan with 450g / 1lb of the sugar and let them remain thus for at least 12 hours. When ready, place the pan on the stove and stew gently until the juice is extracted. Pare, core and cut the apples into thick slices. Add them to the preserving-pan, strain in the juice, add the rest of the sugar, and boil gently from 45 to 50 minutes. Pour into jars, cover closely, and store in a dry, cool place.

APPLE GINGER I

2.25g / 5lb sour apples
1.8kg / 8lb granulated sugar
50g / 2oz fresh ginger root, roughly chopped
1.25ml / ¼ tsp cayenne
3 lemons
600ml / 1 pint cold water

Peel, core and cut the apples into quarters. Dissolve 900g / 2lb of the sugar in 600ml / 1 pint of water, bring slowly to boiling-point, skim well and simmer for 8 or 10 minutes. Pour the syrup over the prepared apples, cover, and let it remain thus for 48 hours. When ready, drain off the syrup into a preserving-pan, add the remaining 900g / 2lb of sugar, the strained juice, and finely-grated rinds of the lemons, the ginger bruised and tied in fine muslin, and the cayenne. When boiling, add the apples, simmer very gently until they are soft, but not broken, then turn into jars. Cover and fasten securely. Store the jars away in a cool, dry place until required for use.

APPLE GINGER II

900g / 2lb sour apples
900g / 2lb granulated sugar
50–100g / 2–4oz fresh ginger root, roughly chopped
900ml / 1½ pints water

Make a syrup of the sugar and water, as directed in the preceding recipe. Meanwhile peel, core, and cut each apple into 8 sections, add them with the ginger root to the syrup, and simmer gently until soft, but not broken. Pour into jars, cover as directed in the preceding recipe, and store in a cool, dry place.

APPLE AND QUINCE JAM

Pare and core an equal number of good apples and quinces. Cut them in pieces, and put them into a pan with 150ml / ¼ pint of water to each 450g / 1lb. Boil them until they are reduced to a pulp, pass them through a sieve, and add 350g / 12oz of sugar to each 450g / 1lb of pulp. Heat gently in a preserving-pan and stir until it is thick and becomes jellied. Decant into dry, clean jars.

APRICOT JAM

Take 1.4kg / 3lb of ripe apricots, pass them through a fine sieve, and add 450g / 1lb of sugar to 450g /1lb of pulp. Heat in a preserving-pan with 300 ml / ½ pint of water and stir well as the mixture boils. After 20 to 30 minutes boiling remove from the heat, add the kernels of the apricots, and then put the jam into clean, dry pots.

APRICOT JAM II

Skin some firm, ripe apricots carefully, break them in halves and remove the stones. Weigh the fruit, and allow an equal amount of fine preserving sugar. Pile the apricots on a large dish, sprinkle each layer with sugar, let them stand for 12 hours, and meanwhile remove the kernels from the stones and blanch them. When ready, place the fruit, sugar and kernels in a preserving-pan, simmer very gently, skimming meanwhile, and as the pieces of apricot become clear remove them from the syrup and place them at once in the pots. Pour on the syrup and kernels, cover closely and store until needed.

BANANA JAM

2.7kg / 6lb bananas
2.3kg / 5lb granulated sugar
900g / 2lb juicy pears
juice 3 lemons

Cut the peeled bananas into small dice and weigh them. Put into the preserving-pan the lemon juice, the pears (peeled and cut up) and 450g / 1lb of the sugar. When boiling put in gradually the bananas and remainder of sugar, stir gently, skim well, and boil for 1 hour. Pour into hot jars and cover.

BARBERRY JAM

Put equal quantities of barberries and preserving sugar into a preserving-pan and bring slowly to boiling point. Boil gently for about 15 or 20 minutes, skimming well and stirring frequently, pour into small pots, cover closely, and store in a cool, dry place.

BLACKBERRY JAM

Boil some blackberries and half their weight in sugar together for 40 minutes. Cover closely, and keep in a dry, cool place. The jam will have a better flavour if a little lemon juice is added.

BLACKCURRANT JAM I

**To each 450g / 1lb fruit allow 450g / 1lb granulated sugar
and 150ml / ¼ pint water**

Remove the fruit, which should be ripe and perfectly dry, from the stalks, put it into a preserving-pan with the water, bring to boiling-point, and simmer gently for 20 minutes. Add the sugar and boil for about half an hour from the time the jam re-boils, or until a little almost immediately sets when tested on a cold plate. Towards the end of the process the jam must be stirred almost continuously to prevent it boiling over or sticking to the bottom of the pan. Pour into pots, cover closely, and store in a cool, dry place until required.

BLACKCURRANT JAM II

**3.6kg / 8lb blackcurrants
1.8kg / 4lb rhubarb
3.6kg / 8lb sugar**

Remove the stalks, pick out the best and finest fruit, place about 2.7kg / 6lb of it on a large dish between layers of sugar, and let it remain for 24 hours. Put the remainder of the currants into a large jar, add the rhubarb previously peeled and cut into short lengths, and cook over a saucepan of boiling water until all the juice is extracted. Of this juice take not less than 900ml / 1½ pints and not more than 1 litre / 2 pints, put it into a large bowl, add the fruit and sugar, and let the whole stand for 24 hours longer.

At the end of this time strain the juice into a preserving-pan, bring to boiling-point, add more sugar if necessary, and boil for about 10 minutes. Now add the fruit, boil gently for 20 minutes, skimming when necessary, then turn the jam into pots, cover closely, and store in a cool, dry place until required.

CARROT JAM I

**To each 450g / 1lb pulp allow 450g / 1lb preserving sugar,
strained juice of 2 lemons, grated rind of 1 lemon,
6 almonds, chopped, 30ml / 2 tbsp brandy**

Wash and scrape the carrots, which must be nice and young, cut each one into 3 or 4 pieces, place them in a preserving-pan with barely sufficient water to cover them, and simmer gently till tender. Drain well, pass through a fine sieve, weigh the pulp, and measure out the preserving sugar, lemon juice and rind, almonds and brandy. Replace the pulp in the preserving-pan with the preserving sugar. Bring slowly to boiling-point, boil for about 5 minutes, stirring and skimming frequently. When cool, add the almonds, brandy, lemon juice and rind, turn into pots, cover closely and store in a cool, dry place. If the brandy be omitted the jam will not keep.

CARROT JAM II
(Imitation apricot)

**Use equal weights of carrots and sugar and to
each 450g / 1lb carrots allow 22.5ml / 1½ tbsp
brandy, juice of 2 lemons, thin rind of 1 lemon and
12 almonds, blanched and quartered**

Scrape and slice the carrots, barely cover them with cold water, simmer slowly until tender, then drain well and pass them through a fine sieve. Replace in the pan, add the sugar, almonds and lemon-juice, boil up, simmer gently for 15 minutes, and stir in the brandy. Turn into pots and store in a dry, cool place. Unless the brandy is added the jam will not keep.

CARROT AND BEETROOT JAM

Use equal weights of carrot and beetroot

Wash the beetroot, scrape the carrots, and boil them separately until tender. Pass through a coarse sieve, measure the pureé, and to each 600ml / 1 pint allow 350g / 12 oz of sugar and the juice of 2 lemons. Place the whole in a preserving-pan, boil gently for half an hour, and turn the preparation into pots. If intended to be kept some time, a glass of brandy should be added to each 600ml / 1 pint of jam before putting it into the pot. Keep closely covered in a dry, cool place.

CHERRY JAM

Use sound, ripe cooking cherries, an equal quantity of preserving sugar and to each 450g / 1lb fruit allow 150ml / ¼ pint redcurrant juice or water, or the two mixed in any proportions

Remove the stones, keeping the cherries as whole as possible, and preserve the kernels. Put the redcurrant juice or water into a preserving-pan with the sugar, and boil to a syrup. Add the cherries and kernels and simmer gently until cherries are tender but not broken and the juice jellies almost immediately when a little is poured on a cold plate. Pour into jars and cover. Store in a cool, dry place.

MICROWAVE TIP

Jam jars may be scalded in the microwave. Half fill perfectly clean jars (without metal trims) with water, place in the microwave and bring the water to the boil on High. Watch the jars closely, turning off the power as soon as the water boils. Carefully remove the jars from the microwave, protecting your hand with an oven glove or tea-towel. Pour away the water, invert the jars on a sheet of absorbent kitchen paper and leave to dry. Fill with jam while still hot.

MORELLO CHERRY JAM

*Cherries are poor in pectin and need a little help is they
are to set properly. In the recipe below, commercially
produced pectin is used.*

**1kg / 2¼lb Morello cherries, stoned
45ml / 3tbsp lemon juice
1.4kg / 3lb sugar
1 (227ml / 8 fl oz) bottle pectin**

Wash the cherries and put them in a preserving pan with the lemon juice.
Add 200ml / 7 fl oz water. Bring to the boil, lower the heat, cover and simmer
for 15 minutes.

Remove the lid, add the sugar and stir over low heat until dissolved. Bring to
the boil and boil rapidly for 3 minutes. Remove from the heat again, skim if
necessary and stir in the pectin thoroughly.

Cool for 15 minutes, pot and cover with waxed paper discs. Put on lids and
labels when cold.

DAMSON JAM I

**To each 450g / 1lb damsons allow from 350–450g /
12oz–1lb preserving sugar, according to taste**

Remove the stalks, put the fruit and sugar into a preserving-pan, simmer gently
until some of the juice is extracted, then bring slowly to boiling-point, occasionally stirring meanwhile. Boil gently for about 45 minutes, or until the syrup,
when tested on a cold plate, stiffens readily. Pour into pots and cover.

DAMSON JAM II

To each 450g / 1lb fruit allow 450g / 1lb sugar

Remove the stalks, put the fruit into a preserving-pan, simmer gently until a little of the juice is extracted, then boil them for half an hour. Now add the sugar gradually, and boil for 20 minutes longer, reckoning from the time the jam re-boils. It must be frequently stirred and if preferred, some or all the stones may be removed before turning the jam into the pots. Cover closely.

GINGER JAM
(Imitation)

24 sticks well-grown rhubarb, or a corresponding
quantity of stalks of lettuce going to seed
preserving sugar
ground ginger
granulated sugar

Remove the outside stringy part, and cut the stalks into 5-cm / 2-inch lengths. Put them into a preserving-pan with 2.2 litres / 4 pints of cold water, 450g / 1lb of preserving sugar, and 15ml / 1 heaped tbsp of ground ginger. Bring slowly to boiling-point, simmer for about 20 minutes, then turn the whole into a bowl and leave, loosely covered, in a cool, dry place.

On the following day drain the juice into the preserving-pan and, when boiling, add the stalks and simmer gently for about half an hour. Repeat this process on the two following days, then drain the stalks and weigh them. To each 450g / 1lb allow 40g / 1½ oz ground ginger, 450g / 1lb granulated sugar, and 900ml / 1½ pints cold water. Boil these together to the 'large thread' degree (103°C / 217°F), and pour the syrup over the stalks. When cold, put the preparation into jars, cover closely, and store in a cool, dry place for about 3 weeks, when it will be ready to use.

GOOSEBERRY JAM

**To each 450g / 1lb gooseberries allow
450g / 1lb preserving sugar and
300ml / ½ pint cold water**

Top and tail the gooseberries. Dissolve the sugar in the cold water, boil up, simmer for about 15 minutes, and remove the scum as it rises. Now put in the fruit, boil gently from 35 to 40 minutes, or until the jam sets readily when tested on a cold plate. Pour into pots, cover, and store in a cool, dry place.

GOOSEBERRY AND CURRANT JAM

**2.7kg / 6lb gooseberries
1.8kg / 4lb preserving sugar
300ml / ½ pint currant juice
*(see Redcurrant Jelly, page 60)***

Head and tail the gooseberries, put them into a preserving-pan, and simmer gently until some of the juice is extracted. Bring to boiling point; when the gooseberries have boiled for 10 minutes add the sugar gradually, put in the redcurrant juice, and boil until the jam sets when tested on a cold plate. The scum must be removed as it rises, and the jam should be well stirred towards the end of the boiling process. When ready pour into pots, cover closely and store in a cool, dry place.

MRS BEETON'S TIP

*When filling jars, stand on
a sheet of newspaper to
catch any drips.*

GRAPE JAM

**To each 450g / 1lb firm, sound, unripe grapes
allow 225g / ½ lb preserving sugar**

Place the fruit and sugar in layers in a preserving-pan, gently simmer until the whole mass is thoroughly hot and some of the juice is extracted, then bring slowly to boiling-point. Boil until the juice sets quickly when tested on a cold plate, pour into small pots, cover closely, and keep in a cool, dry place.

Note: In France, about 100g / 4oz of apples are added to each 450g / 1lb of grapes.

GREEN FIG JAM

**900g / 2lb figs
675g / 1½lb sugar
300ml / ½ pint water
juice of 1 lemon**

Boil the water, sugar, and lemon juice together for 10 minutes, then wipe and slice the fruit, and add it to the syrup. Boil gently for about 1 hour, or until a little of the syrup poured on to a cold plate quickly jellies. Turn into pots, cover and store in a dry place.

GREENGAGE JAM I

**To each 450g / 1lb firm, sound greengages,
allow 350g / 12oz preserving sugar**

Remove the stalks and stones, crack a few of the latter, and put the kernels aside. Cover the bottom of a preserving-pan to the depth of 1cm / ½ inch with cold water, put in the fruit and kernels, bring slowly to boiling-point, and boil gently for about 15 minutes. Meanwhile, place the sugar in the oven in a deep tin or dish, and allow to become thoroughly hot. It may now be added gradually to the fruit, and the boiling must be continued until the jam sets quickly when tested on a cold plate. Pour into pots, cover, and store in a cool, dry place.

GREENGAGE JAM II

Take 1.4kg / 3lb of ripe greengages, extract the stones, and add 1.1kg / 2½ lb of sugar. Put them over a high heat, boil for 20 to 30 minutes, remove them from the heat, add the kernels, and finish as for apricot jam.

MRS BEETON'S TIP

*Ripe or very juicy fruit will need very little
water and only a short cooking time; firmer
varieties may take as long as 20 minutes
to break down and will require up to
250ml / 8 fl oz water.*

GREEN TOMATO PRESERVE

2.7kg / 6lb green tomatoes
3.6kg / 8lb preserving sugar
4 lemons
3 pieces ginger
45ml / 3 tbsp brandy

Cover the tomatoes with water and boil very gently until the tomatoes are soft but unbroken. Drain the water into another pan, add the sugar to it and boil to a syrup. Strain when cold, replace in the pan, add the thinly-pared lemon rind and ginger tied together in muslin, lemon juice and tomatoes. Boil gently until a little of the syrup jellies quickly when poured on to a cold plate, then stir in the brandy. Turn into pots, cover and store in a dry place.

LEMON CURD

4 eggs
450g / 1lb caster sugar
100g / 4oz butter
rind and juice 4 lemons

Break the eggs separately into a basin, beat slightly, add the other ingredients and stir over a gentle heat in a bowl over a pan of hot water for about 20 minutes, or until thick. Pour into dry jars, cover down securely, and store in a cold, dry place.

ORANGE CURD

Substitute 2 oranges and add the juice of 1 lemon. Use only 50g / 2oz butter, melting it in the double saucepan or bowl before adding the rind, juices and sugar.

LOGANBERRY JAM

1.4kg / 3lb loganberries
450g / 1lb raspberries, blackberries or redcurrants
1.8kg / 4lb preserving sugar
600ml / 1 pint water

Prepare fruit and place in a preserving-pan with the sugar. Add the water and cook slowly, skimming occasionally, until the fruit is tender and sets if a little is put onto a cold plate.

If preferred the loganberries may first be partly cooked in the water and then boiled with the other ingredients for about half an hour. In either case, as soon as the jam is sufficiently cooked, pour it into clean dry jars, cover, and store in a cool place.

MIRABELLE JAM

1.4kg / 3lb ripe Mirabelle plums
1.1kg / 2½lb sugar

Extract the stones from the plums, add the sugar, and bring to the boil. Boil for about 25 minutes, then remove them from the heat, place in dry jars, cover and store.

PEACH JAM

**1.8kg / 4lb small firm peaches, peeled and quartered
(see Mrs Beeton's Tip)
5ml / 1 tsp tartaric acid
1.5kg / 3½lb sugar**

Combine the fruit, with the stones, and tartaric acid in a preserving pan. Add 300ml / 1 pint water, bring to the boil, lower the heat and simmer until the fruit is tender. Add the sugar and stir over gentle heat until dissolved. Bring to the boil and boil rapidly, removing the stones as they rise to the surface. Test for set after about 10 minutes of rapid boiling. When ready, remove from the heat skim, pot, cover and label.

MRS BEETON'S TIP

*To peel peaches, place them in a heatproof
bowl, pour on boiling water to cover and leave
for 30 seconds. Drain, cut a small cross in the
top of each fruit and peel away the skin.
Do this just before using the peaches, as
they will discolour if allowed to stand.*

PLUM JAM

**To each 450g / 1lb plums allow 350–450g / 12–16oz
preserving sugar, according to the degree of sweetness
required, and the amount of acidity in the plums**

Divide the plums, take out the stones, or, if preferred, cut them across and remove the stones as they rise in the pan. Pile the fruit on a large dish with the sugar spread thickly between each layer, allow them to remain thus until the following day, then put the whole into a preserving-pan, and simmer gently to release the juice, stirring occasionally meanwhile. Boil gently until the jam sets quickly when tested on a cold plate, then turn it into pots, cover closely, and keep it in a cool, dry place.

MRS BEETON'S TIP

*A stone basket, clipped to the side of the preserving
pan, may be used to hold the stones while allowing
the juice to drip back into the pan. A metal sieve,
hooked over one side of the pan and supported by
the handle on the other, performs equally well.*

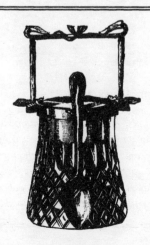

PRUNE JAM

900g / 2lb prunes
finely grated rind and juice of 2 lemons
800g / 1¾ lb sugar

Wash and soak the prunes overnight in about 1.4 litres / 2¼ pints cold water and boil in a clean pan for about half an hour. Remove the prunes and stone them. Put the liquid in a preserving-pan with the lemon rind, lemon juice and sugar, and boil until a thick syrup is obtained. Next, add the prunes and allow them to cook slowly until quite tender. When sufficiently boiled, the jam when tested on a cold plate should set. Pour into clean dry pots, cover and store in a cool place. If liked, some of the stones of the prunes may be cracked and the kernels peeled and mixed with the jam.

QUEENSLAND HONEY FRUIT COMPOTE

225g / 8oz dried prunes
225g / 8oz dried apricots
225g / 8oz dried figs
225g / 8oz dried peaches
275g / 10oz clear honey
600ml / 1 pint water
thinly pared rind 1 lemon

Soak the fruits in water for 8 hours. Drain. Dissolve the honey in the water and boil, together with the lemon rind, for 5 minutes. Remove the rind.

Pack the fruits into sterilized preserving jars. Cover with the syrup to within 1cm / ½ inch of the top of the jars. Stand the jars on a rack in a deep preserving pan and add warm water to come level with the neck of the jars. Bring to the boil and boil for 3 minutes to expel the air from the jars. Cover with the lids, and screw down to seal. Continue boiling for 25 minutes. Remove the jars to a wire rack to cool.

RAISIN PRESERVE

*The fruit may be boiled down for about 1½ hours to make
a very sweet, dark fruit cheese. This lighter recipe,
pepped up with rum, is ideal for winter preserving sessions.
The preserve is good with pancakes or scones.*

450g / 1lb raisins
50g / 2oz candied citron peel, chopped
10ml / 2 tsp ground cinnamon
1.25ml / ¼ tsp ground cloves
225g / 8oz sugar
75ml / 3 fl oz rum

Mix the raisins and citron peel in a large bowl. Add 150ml / ¼ pint water, the
cinnamon, cloves and sugar. Mix well, then cover the bowl and leave to stand
for 24 hours, stirring occasionally. Tip the raisin mixture into a saucepan, scrap-
ing in all the juices from the bowl. Heat gently, stirring until any remaining
sugar has dissolved. Bring to the boil, lower the heat and cover the pan, then
simmer steadily for 30 minutes. Mash the raisins with a potato masher to crush
some of them. Stir in the rum, cover the pan again, then cook for a further
5 minutes. Stir well and pot, pressing the fruit down. Cover at once.

RASPBERRY JAM

To each 450g / 1lb raspberries allow
450g / 1lb sugar and 300 ml / ½ pint redcurrant juice

Let the fruit for this preserve be gathered in fine weather, and used as soon after
it is picked as possible. Take off the stalks, put the raspberries into a preserving-
pan, break them well with a wooden spoon, and let them boil for about half an
hour, keeping them well stirred. Add the redcurrant juice and sugar, and boil
again for half an hour. Skim the jam well after the sugar is added, or the
preserve will not be clear. The addition of the currant juice is a very great
improvement to this preserve.

REDCURRANT JAM

To each 450g / 1lb redcurrants allow
350g / 12oz preserving sugar

Remove the stalks from the currants, put the fruit into a preserving-pan, and add the sugar. Stir occasionally until the fruit is nearly boiling, and afterwards almost continuously. Boil gently for about 40 minutes, or until a little will set when poured on to a cold plate. Turn into pots, cover closely, and store in a cool dry place.

RED AND WHITECURRANT JAMS

Pick the currants, put them in a preserving-pan over a medium heat, and stir until mashed. Then pass them through sieve, add 450g / 1lb of sugar to an equal weight of pulp, and finish as for Apricot Jam (page 14).

RHUBARB JAM

To each 450g / 1lb rhubarb allow 450g / 1lb preserving sugar,
5ml / 1 tsp ground ginger, and the
finely-grated rind of ½ lemon

Remove the outer stringy part of the rhubarb, cut it into short lengths, and weigh it. Put it into a preserving-pan with sugar, ginger, and lemon rind in the above proportions, place the pan over a medium heat and let the contents come very slowly to boiling-point, stirring occasionally meanwhile. Boil until the jam sets quickly when tested on a cold plate. Pour it into pots, cover closely, and store.

RHUBARB AND ORANGE JAM

1 litre / 2 pints finely-cut rhubarb
6 oranges
675g / 1½lb preserving sugar

Cut the rinds of the oranges into sections, remove them and scrape off as much of the white pith as possible. Free the pulp from fibrous skin and pips, put it into a preserving-pan, with the sugar, rhubarb and orange rinds, previously finely-shredded. Bring slowly to boiling-point, skim well, and boil until the jam stiffens when tested on a cold plate. Cover closely, and store in a cool, dry place.

STRAWBERRY JAM

To each 450g / 1lb strawberries allow
350–450g / 12 to 16 oz preserving sugar

Remove the stalks from the fruit, put it into a preserving-pan, covering each layer thickly with sugar. Bring the contents slowly to boiling point, and stir occasionally. Skim well, boil gently until the jam sets when tested on a cold plate, taking care in stirring to keep the fruit as whole as possible. Pour into pots, cover, and keep in a cool, dry place.

MICROWAVE TIP

Small amounts of strawberry jam can be successfully made in the microwave. The jam will have very good colour and flavour but will only be lightly set. Put 450g / 1lb hulled strawberries in a large, deep mixing bowl; the mixture rises considerably while cooking. Add 450g / 1lb sugar and mix lightly. Cover and allow to stand overnight. Next day, uncover and cook on High until setting point is reached, stirring occasionally and checking for setting every 10 minutes. Remove from the microwave, using oven gloves to protect your hands. Leave to stand, then pot.
Makes about 675g / 1½lb.

WHOLE STRAWBERRY JAM

1.5 kg / 3¼ lb strawberries, hulled
juice of 1 lemon
1.5 kg / 3¼ lb sugar

Combine the strawberries and lemon juice in a preserving pan. Heat gently for 10 minutes, stirring all the time to reduce the volume. Add the sugar, stirring over low heat until it has dissolved.

Bring to the boil and boil rapidly until setting point is reached. Remove from the heat and skim. Leave the jam undisturbed to cool for about 20 minutes or until a skin firms on the surface and the fruit sinks. Stir gently to distribute the strawberries. Pot and top with waxed paper discs. Cover and label when cold.

TOMATO JAM

To each 450g / 1lb ripe tomatoes allow 450g / 1lb sugar

Scald the tomatoes and remove the skins. Cut open the fruit and remove the seeds. Put the fruit and sugar together in a pan, and add the juice of 2 lemons to every 1.4kg / 3lb fruit and sugar, and 5ml / 1 tsp ground ginger. Crush the fruit with a wooden spoon, and mix the whole well together. Boil slowly for about 2 hours, keeping it well stirred and skimmed.

VEGETABLE MARROW JAM I

**To each 450g / 1lb marrow
allow 450g / 1lb granulated sugar**

Take some young marrows, peel them, remove the seeds, cut into thin slices and then into fine shreds. Make a syrup with 50g / 1lb of Demerara sugar to 600ml / 1 pint of water. When it is boiling, pour it over the marrows and let them soak for 2 days and 2 nights in a covered jar or a basin, then strain off the syrup. Add the granulated sugar, rind and juice of 1 lemon and 25g / 1oz of whole ginger tied up in muslin. Place in a pan, boil slowly until clear, then add a small glass of whisky or brandy (optional). Pour into jars, cover, and set in a cool place.

Note: Allow 2.2 litres / 4 pints of syrup to 2.7kg / 6lb of fruit.

VEGETABLE MARROW JAM II

**To each pound of marrow allow
350g / 12oz preserving sugar**

Peel and slice the marrow; remove the seeds. Place the sugar in alternate layers with the sliced marrow, and leave undisturbed for at least 12 hours. When ready, boil gently for about an hour, then add 5ml / 1 tsp ginger to each 1.8kg / 4lb marrow, stir until well mixed, and turn into jars; cover, and store in a dry place.

MRS BEETON'S TIP

*Vegetable marrow jam will not produce a
definite set. It is potted when it reaches the
desired volume and consistency.*

VEGETABLE MARROW PRESERVE

**To each 450g / 1lb marrow
allow 450g / 1lb granulated sugar
50g / 2oz root or stem ginger
rind and juice of 4 lemons**

Take 3 or 4 young vegetable marrows weighing about 2.7kg / 6lb. Peel them rather thinly, cut in half, and remove the seeds, then cut each half into thick slices and subsequently into dice or cubes. Put the vegetable marrow, and its weight in granulated sugar, into a preserving-pan with 1 litre / 2 pints of water. Boil gently for about 20 minutes; pour into a bowl and return all the liquid to the pan. Add 50g / 2oz of root or stem ginger previously bruised and tied in a piece of muslin, add also the thinly-cut rind and strained juice of 4 lemons. Boil for about half an hour; then add the marrow and boil up, skim and cook gently for another half an hour. Remove the ginger, fill the preserve into jars, and cover in the usual manner.

Marmalades

*The quintessential partner for toast at breakfast,
this chapter includes the ever-popular
coarse-cut and clear orange marmalades
alongside more unusual recipes.*

APPLE MARMALADE

900g / 2lb apples
100g / 4oz sugar
25g / 1oz butter

Peel, core and quarter the apples, place them in a jar with the sugar and butter, and stand the jar in a saucepan containing boiling water, or, when more convenient, in a cool oven. Cook until soft, pass through a fine sieve, and use for filling turnovers or other kinds of pastry.

FIVE FRUIT MARMALADE

1kg / 2¼lb fruit (1 orange, 1 grapefuit, 1 lemon
1 large cooking apple, 1 pear)
1.5kg / 3¼lb sugar

Wash the citrus fruit, peel it, scrape off the pith and shred the peel finely. Chop the flesh roughly. Put the pips, pith and any coarse tissue into a bowl with 500ml / 18 fl oz water. Put the peel and chopped flesh in a second, larger bowl with 1.5 litres / 2¾ pints water. Leave both mixtures to soak for 24 hours. Line a strainer with muslin and strain the liquid containing the pips into a preserving-pan. Bring up the sides of the muslin and tie to make a bag containing the pith and pips. Add the bag to the pan, along with the contents of the second bowl. Peel and dice the apple and pear and add to the pan.

MRS BEETON'S TIP

If a very clear jelly is required,
do not squeeze the muslin bag;
instead tie it to the handle and
allow the liquid to drip slowly
back into the pan.

THE ORIGINAL MARMALADE

Records show that a preserve called 'marmalade', made from the marmelo or quince, was imported into Britain from Portugal before the sixteenth century. Quinces had long been used in physicians' recipes, and were thought to aid digestion. Before the sixteenth century preserves were always referred to as marmalades of damsons or whatever fruit was used. But by the early 1500s the word was only used to mean a preserve of quinces. The first recipe for marmalade to be published in English appeared in 1562 and gave instructions for a quince pulp to be boiled with sugar and flavoured with spices.

Bring the liquid to the boil, lower the heat and simmer for 1¼ hours or until the volume is reduced by one third. Remove from the heat. Squeeze the muslin bag over the pan to extract as much of the pectin-rich juice as possible.

Return the pan to the heat, add the sugar and stir over a low heat until dissolved. Bring to the boil and boil rapidly for about 30 minutes or until the setting point is reached. Remove from the heat and skim quickly.

Leave to cool slightly until a skin forms on the surface of the marmalade, then stir, pot and top with waxed paper discs. Cover and label when cold.

GRAPE MARMALADE

Remove the grape stalks, put the fruit into a preserving-pan, barely cover with boiling water, and simmer gently until perfectly soft, but the grapes must not be allowed to break. Drain well, pass through a fine sieve, and return the pulp to the pan. To each 600ml / 1 pint add from 350g–450g / 12–16oz of preserving sugar, according to degree of sweetness required, and boil from 20 to 25 minutes, reckoning from the time the entire mass reaches boiling point. Turn into jars, cover, and store in a cool, dry place.

GRAPEFRUIT MARMALADE

1kg / 2¼lb grapefruit
3 lemons
2kg / 4½lb sugar

Wash the fruit and cut it in half. Squeeze it and strain the juice into a large bowl. Reserve the fruit shells, pulp and pips.

Scrape any thick pith from the shells and tie it in a muslin bag with the pips. Shred the peel finely and add it to the bowl of juice, with the muslin bag. Add 2 litres / 4½ pints water and leave overnight to soften and bring out the flavour.

Next day, transfer the contents of the bowl to a preserving pan. Bring the liquid to the boil, lower the heat and simmer for 2 hours or until the peel is tender. Remove from the heat. Squeeze the muslin bag over the pan to extract all the juice.

Return the pan to the heat, add the sugar and stir until it has dissolved. Bring to the boil and boil fast until the setting point is reached. Remove from the heat and skim quickly. Leave to cool slightly until a skin forms on the surface of the marmalade, then stir, pot and top with waxed paper discs. Cover and label when cold.

PRESSURE COOKER TIP

To adapt this recipe, reduce the quantity of water to 1 litre / 2 pints. Combine the juice, peel, water and muslin bag in the base of the cooker, bring to 15lb pressure and cook for 8 minutes. Reduce the pressure quickly and remove the muslin bag. Return the open cooker to heat, add sugar and finish as above.

GRAPEFRUIT AND PINEAPPLE MARMALADE

450g / 1lb grapefruit
1 small pineapple
juice 1 lemon
1.5kg / 3¼lb sugar

Wash the grapefruit, peel it, scrape off the pith and shred the peel finely. Cut up the flesh roughly, putting the pips, coarse tissue and pith to one side. Measure the total volume of fruit and peel: it should equal 750ml / 1¼ pints. Put the flesh and peel in a bowl with 1 litre / 1¾ pints water. Combine the pips, coarse tissue and pith in a second bowl and add 500ml / 18fl oz water. Leave both mixtures to soak for 24 hours.

Next day, line a strainer with muslin and strain the liquid containing the pips into a preserving-pan. Bring up the sides of the muslin and tie to make a bag containing the pith and pips. Add the bag to the pan, with the contents of the second bowl.

Cut the pineapple into slices, removing the skin, eyes and hard core; chop the flesh into small pieces. Measure the pineapple with the lemon juice; there should be 250ml / 8 fl oz. Add the mixture to the preserving-pan.

Bring the liquid to the boil, lower the heat and simmer until the volume is reduced by one third. Remove from the heat; squeeze out the muslin bag. Return the pan to the heat, add the sugar and stir over a low heat until dissolved. Bring to the boil and boil rapidly for about 30 minutes or until the setting point is reached. Remove from the heat and skim quickly.

Leave to cool slightly until a skin forms on the surface of the marmalade, then stir, pot and top with waxed paper discs. Cover and label when cold.

GRATED MARMALADE

12 large Seville oranges
2 lemons
preserving sugar

Grate the rinds of 6 oranges, remove all the white pith, and throw it away. Remove and throw away both rind and pith of the remaining 6 oranges. Weigh the oranges, and to each 450g / 1lb allow 450g / 1lb of sugar. Divide into sections, scrape out the pulp, and soak the pips and pith in a little cold water. Place the sugar, juice of the 2 lemons, orange-rind, pulp and juice in a preserving-pan, add the water strained from the pips and pitch, and boil gently until the marmalade jellies quickly when tested on a cold plate. Cover the jars closely, and store them in a dry, cool place.

KUMQUAT CONSERVE

575g / 1¼lb kumquats
1 lemon
400g / 14oz sugar

Slice the kumquats in half and remove the pips, setting them aside. Peel the lemon, then roughly chop the flesh, setting aside the pips and any coarse tissue or pith. Tie all the trimmings in a muslin bag and put the kumquats and lemon flesh in a large saucepan. Add the muslin bag and pour in 400ml / 14 fl oz water.

Bring to the boil, lower the heat, cover the pan and simmer for 30 minutes or until the kumquats feel tender when pierced. Squeeze out the muslin bag over the pan.

Stir in the sugar trying not break up the fruit. Cook gently, stirring until all the sugar has dissolved, then boil until the setting point is reached.

Remove from the heat and skim quickly, if necessary. Leave to cool slightly until a skin forms on top, then stir, pot, and top with waxed paper discs. Cover and label when cold.

LEMON MARMALADE I

Place the lemons in a preserving-pan, cover them with cold water, and boil them gently for about 2 hours, during which time the water must be drained off and replaced by fresh boiling water at least three times. Let the cool slightly, slice thinly, remove all the pips, and weigh the fruit. To each 450g / 1lb allow 900g / 2lb of granulated sugar and 600ml / 1 pint of the water the lemons were last boiled in, and boil these together until a thin syrup is obtained. Then add the prepared fruit, and boil until the marmalade jellies when tested on a cold plate. Cover closely and store in a cool, dry place.

LEMON MARMALADE II

Prepare the lemons as directed in the preceding recipe, then weigh them. Take an equal weight of sour cooking apples, pare, core, slice them, and stew them gently until reduced to a pulp. Add the weight of the apple pulp to that of the sliced lemons; to each 450g / 1lb allow 900g / 2lb of preserving sugar, and 600ml / 1 pint of the water the lemons were last boiled in. Boil the sugar and water to a thin syrup, add the fruit, and boil gently until the marmalade sets quickly when tested on a cold plate. Pour into pots, cover and store in a cool, dry place.

LEMON MARMALADE III

900g / 2lb lemons
1.8kg / 4lb granulated sugar

Choose the lemons so that they are clear and smooth. Put them in a copper preserving-pan, and cover well with water, boil them for about 2 hours, changing the water two or three times during the process. Drain them, keep the water the lemons were last boiled in. Cut the lemons in halves longways, and slice them as finely as possible, removing all the pips. Take 3 pints of the lemon water and put it with the sugar on to boil. Remove the scum, and let boil for about 15 minutes. Add the fruit and boil again until it becomes clear. Strain off the fruit when cold, boil up the syrup again, add the fruit, give it another boil, then put into jars, let it cool and cover, and store in the usual manner.

ORANGE MARMALADE I

12 Seville oranges
2 lemons
preserving sugar

Slice the fruit thinly, removing inner pith and pips. Weigh it, and to each 450g / 1lb add 3 pints of cold water. Leave, covered, in a bowl for 3 days, then turn the preparation into a preserving-pan and boil gently until quite tender. Let it cool, weigh again, and to each 450g / 1lb of fruit add 450g / 1lb of sugar. Bring to boiling-point, skim well, and cook gently until the syrup stiffens quickly when tested on a cold plate. Turn into pots, cover and store in a cool, dry place.

ORANGE MARMALADE II

24 Seville oranges
preserving sugar
1 litre / 2 pints cold water.

Weigh the oranges and measure out an equal amount of preserving sugar. Remove the rinds of the oranges, divide the pulp into small pieces, and remove the pips. Boil the rinds in water for 2 hours, changing it two or three times to reduce the bitter flavour; when quite tender, drain well, and shred them finely. Boil the sugar and water to a syrup, skimming well meanwhile, then add the pulp and shredded rinds. Boil gently for about half an hour, or until the marmalade sets quickly when tested on a cold plate, then pour into pots and cover. Keep the marmalade in a cool, dry place until required for use.

ORANGE MARMALADE III

(Transparent)

1.8kg / 4lb Seville oranges
3.6kg / 8lb preserving sugar
3.4 litres / 6 pints water
2 or 3 egg whites

Remove the rinds of the oranges, and scrape away the white pith. Shred the rind finely, cover with water, boil gently until tender, then strain and preserve the liquid. Strip every particle of pith from the oranges, slice them, and remove the pips, and soak these in a little cold water. Simmer the remainder of the water and the sliced oranges for about 2 hours, then drain through a fine sieve or cloth, but do not squeeze the pulp. Replace the liquid in the pan, add the liquid in which the rind was cooked and the strained water from the pips, bring nearly to boiling-point, and clarify with white of eggs. Strain until the syrup jellies when tested on a cold plate, and add the orange rind. Simmer gently for some 10 minutes longer, then turn into pots, cover closely, and store in a dry, cool place.

ORANGE MARMALADE WITH HONEY

Boil the rinds of some oranges until tender, then shred them finely. Remove the pith and pips, measure the pulp, and to each 600ml / 1 pint allow 450g / 1lb of honey and 225g / ½lb of the prepared rinds. Simmer gently for about 40 minutes, stirring frequently, then turn the marmalade into jars, and cover. Store the jars away in a cool, dry place.

PEACH AND PINEAPPLE MARMALADE

3.2kg / 7lb peaches
1 large ripe pineapple
3 lemons
2.7kg / 6lb sugar

Pare and slice the pineapple, peel and stone the peaches, crack half the stones and remove the kernels. Put the peaches and pineapple into a preserving-pan with just a little water to protect the bottom layer, heat slowly to simmering point, and afterwards cook gently for about half an hour. Add the sugar gradually, so as not to reduce the temperature below simmering point, the strained juice of the lemons and the kernels, and boil gently for about 20 minutes, skimming when necessary. Pour into jars, cover closely, and store in a cool, dry place.

PINEAPPLE MARMALADE

Peel, core and slice the pineapples, and either pound or grate them finely, preferably the latter. To each 450g / 1lb of pulp add 400g / 14oz of granulated sugar. Boil the pulp and sugar together until thick and clear, then turn into pots. Store in a cool, dry place.

QUINCE MARMALADE

Pare the fruit, put it into a preserving-pan with as much water as will just cover the bottom of the pan, and stew gently until reduced to a pulp. Pass through a fine sieve, weigh the pulp, replace it in the pan, and to each 450g / 1lb of pulp add 450g / 12oz of preserving sugar, and cook very gently until the marmalade sets quickly when tested on a cold plate. Pot and store in a cool, dry place.

MRS BEETON'S TIP

If the quinces are very hard, they may be grated or minced coarsely, in which case the amount of water used should be doubled.

TANGERINE MARMALADE

30 tangerines
granulated or preserving sugar
6 lemons

Wash the tangerines in water and wipe them. Weigh the tangerines, then measure out double their weight in sugar. Place them in a preserving-pan with enough cold water to float them, and let them boil till the rinds are soft. Drain off the water. Cut each tangerine in quarters, remove the pips, place in a basin containing a pint of cold water, and let them soak for 12 hours. Remove all the pulp from the rind, and mash it well, slice the peel as thinly as possible. Put the sugar in a preserving-pan with the water from the pips, and the strained juice of the lemons. Reduce this to the consistency of thick syrup, then add the tangerine pulp and rinds, and boil for about half an hour. Fill into jars, and when cold cover them.

Note: Before removing the marmalade from the heat, pour a little on a plate which should set like jelly when cold, if not, reduce it a little longer.

THREE FRUIT MARMALADE

This popular marmalade combines the flavours of grapefruit, orange and lemon.

1 grapefruit
2 lemons
1 sweet orange
1.5kg / 3½lb sugar

Wash the citrus fruit, peel it, scrape off the pith and shred the peel finely or coarsely as preferred. Chop the flesh roughly. Tie the pips, pith and any coarse tissue in a muslin bag. Put the peel, chopped flesh and muslin bag in a large bowl, add 2 litres / 3½ pints water and soak for 24 hours.

Next day, transfer the contents of the bowl to a preserving pan. Bring the liquid to the boil, lower the heat and simmer for 1½ hours or until the peel is tender and the contents of the bag are reduced by one third. Remove from the heat. Squeeze the muslin bag over the pan to extract as much of the juice as possible.

Return the pan to the heat, add the sugar and stir over a low heat until dissolved. Bring to the boil and boil rapidly until the setting point is reached. Remove from the heat and skim quickly.

Leave to cool slightly until a skin forms on the surface of the marmalade, then stir, pot and top with waxed paper discs. Cover and label when cold.

MRS BEETON'S TIP

The quickest method of preparing fruit for marmalade is to opt for a chunky style preserve then simply wash and chop the whole fruit, discarding pips as you work.

TOMATO MARMALADE

3.2kg / 7lb ripe tomatoes
3.6kg / 8lb granulated sugar
300ml / ½ pint water
6 lemons

Remove the stalks from the tomatoes, wipe them with a cloth, blanch, skin, and cut each into halves; peel the lemons, cut them into slices, and remove the pips. Put the sugar and water into a preserving-pan, stir gently over the heat until the sugar is dissolved, skim, and boil to a syrup; put in the tomatoes and lemons and boil quickly, stirring from time to time. Remove the scum which rises to the top. When done, pour into jars, cover and store.

MRS BEETON'S TIP

Central heating poses special problems when it comes to keeping preserves in good condition.
It is a good idea to use the modern twist top jam jars which can create an airtight seal when closed immediately after potting.

Fruit Jellies

*Sparkling jellies in clear pots look beautiful
and make excellent accompaniments to
both sweet and savoury foods.*

Fruit jellies are prepared with juices from fruits containing pectin or vegetable jelly with the addition of an equal quantity of sugar.

The best fruits, and those most adapted for making jellies, are redcurrants, gooseberries, apples, quinces, Seville oranges, etc.

Care should be taken not to boil jellies too much; for if they are over boiled their colour is spoiled, and they become ropy, like treacle.

APPLE JELLY I

All sour or tart apples make excellent jelly. Wash the apples and remove all unsound parts. Cut them into pieces without paring or removing the core. Place in a preserving-pan, add enough water to cover, and cook till tender. Drain the juice, and allow 350g / 12oz of granulated sugar to each 600ml / 1 pint. Measure 1.7 litres / 3 pints of juice into the preserving-pan, boil about 15 minutes, then add the sugar and cook till it forms a jelly when cold.

APPLE JELLY II

4.5kg / 10lb apples
5 pints water
sugar
lemons

Rub the apples well with a dry cloth, but do not pare them. Cut them into quarters, remove the cores, and put them into a preserving-pan with the water. Simmer until perfectly soft, but not broken, then strain off the liquid without squeezing the pulp. If not clear, pass through a jelly-bag or clean dry cloth, until it becomes so. To each 600ml / 1 pint of liquid obtained allow 450g / 1lb of sugar and the juice of 2 lemons, and simmer gently until a little, poured on a cold plate, almost immediately begins to stiffen. Pour into pots, cover closely, and store in a cool, dry place.

APPLE JELLY III

**To each 2.7kg / 6lb apples allow 1.7 litres / 3 pints water;
to every 1 litre / 2 pints juice allow 900g / 2lb granulated sugar
and the juice of ½ lemon**

Pare, core and cut the apples into slices, and put them into a casserole dish, with water in the above proportion. Place them in a cool oven, with the dish well covered, and when the juice is thoroughly drawn and the apples are quite soft, strain them through a jelly-bag. To each 1 litre / 2 pints of juice allow 900g / 2lb of granulated sugar, which should be crushed to small lumps and put in the preserving-pan with the juice. Boil these together for rather more than half an hour, remove the scum as it rises, add the lemon juice just before it is done, and put the jelly into pots.

APRICOT JELLY

**To each 450g / 1lb ripe apricots, weighed after the stones
and skins are removed, allow 450g / 1lb preserving sugar
and the juice of 1 lemon**

Remove the skins, break the apricots in halves, and blanch the kernels. Weigh the fruit, put it into a preserving-pan with an equal amount of sugar, and add the prepared kernels and lemon-juice. Simmer gently, stir frequently until reduced to the consistency of thick marmalade, then pour into small pots. Cover and store in a dry, cool place.

BARBERRY JELLY

Wash the ripe barberries in cold water, and put them into a dish with a close fitting lid, place the dish on the stove or in a moderate oven, in a tin half full of boiling water, and simmer gently for about 2 hours. Strain the juice into a preserving-pan, to each 600ml / 1 pint add 450g / 1lb of granulated sugar, and bring to boiling point. Boil for about 10 minutes, removing the scum as it rises, then pour into small pots and cover.

BLACKBERRY JELLY

2.7kg / 6lb blackberries
6 medium sized sour apples
juice of 1 lemon
¾ pint water
sugar

Stalk the blackberries, wipe, peel, core and slice the apples. Place the apples, water and lemon juice into a preserving-pan. Cook until the apples are soft, then add the blackberries and continue to boil until they are soft. Strain off the liquid through a fine sieve or cloth. Do not rub the fruit, only press it lightly to extract the juice. Wash out the pan, allow 450g / 1lb of sugar to each 600ml / 1 pint of juice and boil in the pan until it will set if a little is cooled on a plate. Pour it into dry warm jars, cover and store in a cool place.

BLACKCURRANT JELLY

Remove the stalks from the blackcurrants and put the fruit into a bowl placed over a saucepan of boiling water, and simmer until their juice is extracted. Strain the juice into a preserving-pan, to each 600ml / 1 pint add 70ml / 2½ fl oz water and 350g / ¾lb preserving sugar, and boil gently until the jelly stiffens when a little is tested on a cold plate. Pour into small pots, cover and store in a cool, dry place until required for use.

CRAB APPLE JELLY

1.8kg / 4lb crab apples
2.3 litres / 4 pints water
6 cloves
5cm / 1 inch ginger
450g / 1lb sugar to each 600ml / 1 pint of strained liquid

Halve the crab apples with a silver knife. Place them in the water, add the cloves and ginger, simmer until tender, then drain well, but do not squeeze the apples. Replace the drained liquid in the pan, add the sugar, boil until the syrup jellies quickly when tested on a cold plate, then pour into small jars. Cover securely and store in a cool, dry place.

CRANBERRY JELLY

225g / 8oz cranberries
175g / 6oz sugar
pinch soda
5ml / 1 tsp lemon juice
215ml / 7½ fl oz water

Pick over and wash the cranberries, put them in a preserving-pan with the water and soda. Remove the scum as soon as it begins to boil, then add the sugar, and boil gently for about 20 minutes, and keep covered whilst boiling. Remove the lid and add the lemon juice, reduce briskly for a few minutes until the liquid stiffens; strain into a bowl, allow it to set in a cool place, and turn out when required. This makes a very excellent and most appropriate accompaniment with roast turkey.

CHERRY JELLY

Prepare as for Redcurrant Jelly (page 60), measuring the fruit in the proportion of 1.4kg / 3lb of cherries to 450g / 1lb of redcurrants.

DAMSON JELLY

The damsons must be firm, dry and ripe. Remove the stalks, put the fruit into a large jar or stew-pot, cover closely, place it in a boiling-pot of cold water, and cook very slowly until the plums are perfectly tender. Strain the juice through a jelly-bag, or fine cloth, into a preserving-pan, add from 225–275g / 8–10oz of preserving sugar to each 600ml / 1 pint of juice, and boil until the jelly sets quickly when tested on a cold plate. Pour into pots, cover closely and store in a cool, dry place.

GOOSEBERRY JELLY

**To each 300ml / ½ pint gooseberries allow 300ml / ½ pint water;
to each 600ml / pint juice obtained add 450g / 1lb sugar**

Put the fruit and water into a preserving-pan, and boil slowly until reduced to a pulp. Strain through a jelly-bag or fine cloth until clear, then put it into the preserving-pan with the sugar, and boil until it will set when a little is poured on a cold plate. Turn into small pots, cover and store the jelly in a cool, dry place.

GRAPE JELLY

**To each 450g / 1lb grapes allow 150ml / ¼ pint cold water;
to each 600ml / pint juice obtained add 450g / 1lb loaf
or preserving sugar**

Remove the stalks, put the fruit and the water into a preserving-pan, and simmer very gently until the grapes are soft. Strain the juice through a jelly-bag or fine cloth until clear, replace it in the pan, and boil rapidly for about half an hour. Add the sugar and continue the boiling until the jelly sets quickly when tested on a cold plate. As the scum rises it should be carefully removed. When ready pour the jelly into small pots, cover closely, and store in a cool, dry place.

PRESENTING PRESERVES AS GIFTS

• *Cover the tops of jars with brightly coloured fabrics (gingham is traditional) cut into circles large enough to leave about 4cm / 1½ inches overhanging the edge of the pot. Hem the edges or cut with pinking shears and fix in place with coloured elastic bands or satin ribbons bearing a pretty gift tag that tones with the fabric.*

• *Cut similar covers from metallic gift-wrap papers and fix in place.*

• *Decorate glass jars with glass paint – a border around the lower edge, the name of the preserve or a greeting – in colours to tone with the fruit in the jar, or stick silver and gold stars around the outside.*

• *Cut labels of different shapes from colourful paper and attach to the preserve or pot. Write the name of the preserve in coloured ink or with a silver or gold spirit pen.*

MEDLAR JELLY

Put ripe medlars into a preserving-pan after cutting off the tops. Cover with cold water, boil slowly for some hours, then strain off the juice through a fine sieve. Allow about 450g / 1lb of preserving sugar to each 600ml / 1 pint of juice. Boil the juice and sugar together over a high heat, stirring all the time, from 20 to 30 minutes, or until the mixture thickens and is sufficiently set if dropped and cooled on a plate. As soon as the mixture is sufficiently cooled pour it into clean dry jars, cover and store in a cool place.

ORANGE JELLY
(Seville)

Using fine Seville oranges, squeeze out the juice, filter it through a jelly bag or cloth, and proceed and finish as for Redcurrant Jelly (see page 60).

POMEGRANATE JELLY

Mash the seeds of 6 very ripe pomegranates, mix with the juice of 2 oranges and 2 lemons, adding the rind of one. Strain through a cloth or jelly-bag, and finish as for Barberry Jelly (page 52). Pour into the mould a layer of jelly. When it is set, place on it a layer of pomegranate, and then another layer of jelly, and so on until the mould is filled.

PRICKLY PEAR OR CACTUS FRUIT JELLY

1.4kg / 3lb prickly pears or cactus fruit
1.7 litres / 3 pints water
lemons
preserving sugar

Rub off the spines very carefully with a thick cloth. Cut the fruit in half and add the water. Boil till the fruit is almost in a pulp. Strain away the liquid, and for every 600ml / 1 pint allow the juice of a lemon and 450g / 1lb sugar. Simmer gently, removing any scum until the syrup jellies. Cover and store for future use.

PHYSALIS JELLY

Have ready some physalis pods (Cape gooseberries), sugar and lemon juice. Wipe the pods, cover them with cold water, simmer gently until soft, then drain through a jelly-bag, but do not squeeze the pulp. Measure the liquor carefully, and to each 600ml / 1 pint add 450g / 1lb of sugar and 10ml / 2 tsp of lemon juice, and simmer gently for about half an hour, skimming meanwhile. Pour the jelly into jars and cover. The jars should be stored in a cool, dry place.

QUINCE JELLY I

Select the fruit ripe and of fine flavour. The orange quince is considered the best. Wash well and rub the fruit with a cloth. The best part of the quince can be used for bottling and preserving. Make the jelly from the rind and hard knotty parts, with the addition of some of the whole fruit. Remove the seeds or core portion. Cover the fruit with water, stew gently until tender, and then drain; 350g / 12oz sugar to each 600ml / 1 pint of juice is sufficient. Measure 1.7 litres / 3 pints of juice into the preserving-pan, boil for about 15 minutes, add sugar and proceed as previously directed.

QUINCE JELLY II

1.8kg / 4lb quinces – not too ripe
sugar

Slice the quinces into a pan with enough water to cover and boil them until tender. Pour the mixture through a jelly bag or cloth, and for each 600 ml / 1 pint of filtered juice add 350g / 12oz of sugar. Boil for 10 to 20 minutes, remove the scum, and finish as for Redcurrant Jelly (page 60).

QUINCE JELLY III

Pare and slice the quinces, and put them into a preserving-pan with sufficient water to float them. Boil them until the fruit is reduced to a pulp. Strain off the clear juice, and to each 600 ml / 1 pint allow 450g / 1lb granulated sugar. Boil the juice and sugar together for about 45 minutes, remove all the scum as it rises, and when the jelly appears firm upon a little being poured on a plate, pour into small pots. The residue left on the sieve will answer to make a common marmalade for immediate use, by boiling it with 225g / ½lb of sugar to every 450g / 1lb of pulp.

RASPBERRY JELLY

Let the raspberries be freshly gathered, quite ripe, and picked from the stalks; put them into a large jar after breaking the fruit a little with a wooden spoon, and place the jar, covered, in a saucepan of boiling water.

When the juice is well drawn, which will be from 45 minutes to 1 hour, strain the fruit through a fine sieve or cloth, measure the juice, and to each 600ml / 1 pint allow 100g / ¼lb of granulated sugar. Put the juice and sugar into a preserving-pan, place it over the heat, and boil gently until the jelly thickens upon a little being poured on a cold plate; carefully remove all the scum as it rises, pour the jelly into small pots, cover and keep in a dry place.

REDCURRANT JELLY I

1.4kg / 3lb redcurrants
450g / 1lb white currants
sugar

Pick and wash the currants and mash them through a coarse sieve, then put them into a pan with a very little water. Put the pan on the heat, and stir the fruit until it boils. Withdraw from the heat, remove the scum, and pass the juice through a jelly bag or cloth. Measure and boil this for 10 to 15 minutes, add the sugar in equal quantities. Boil again, remove the scum, and put the jelly into clean, dry jars. When cold it should be covered and stored in a cool, dry place.

REDCURRANT JELLY II

Strip the currants from the stalks, place the fruit in a saucepan with a little water and simmer for about half an hour until all the juice is extracted. Then strain through a jelly-bag or fine cloth into a preserving-pan. To each 600ml / 1 pint add 450g / 1lb preserving sugar, and boil slowly for about 45 minutes. Skim well. When the jelly is sufficiently boiled, it will set quickly if a little is put on a cold plate. Pour into small dry pots and cover in the usual way.

WHITE CURRANT JELLY

Pick the currants from the stalk, and put them into a jar. Place the jar in a saucepan of boiling water, simmer gently until the juice is extracted, then strain through a jelly-bag or fine cloth into a preserving-pan. To each 600ml / pint allow from 350g–450g / 12oz–1lb of preserving sugar, according to taste, and boil gently until the jelly quickly sets, when a little is poured on a cold plate. Turn into small pots, cover and keep the jelly in a cool, dry place.

Bottled Fruit

Enjoy seasonal fruits all year. Bottled fruit is delicious in crumbles, pancakes, pies and flans, or try mixing it with whipped double cream to fill gâteaux and meringues.

Bottled produce is preserved by heating. The fruit and liquid in the jar are heated to a high enough temperature and for sufficient time, to kill micro-organisms (bacteria, yeast and moulds). The jar must be sealed while the contents are at a high temperature to prevent any new micro-organisms from entering.

EQUIPMENT

Preserving Jars

Special preserving jars must be used for bottled fruit. They are manufactured to withstand high temperatures and to form an airtight seal when the contents are processed correctly. The jars must be in good condition; any that are chipped, cracked or damaged in any way will not seal properly even if they do withstand the temperature during processing. ·

There are two types of preserving jars: screw band jars or clip jars. Screw bands, made of metal or plastic, usually have a built-in rubber (or plastic) ring which provides the seal. New screw bands or sealing rings may be purchased and they should be replaced after each use. Screw bands should be loosened by a quarter turn before processing to allow for expansion when the jars are heated.

Clip jars have metal clips and separate rubber rings to seal the lids. The rubber rings should be replaced each time they are used, otherwise they will not seal the jar properly. Old, unused rubber rings should not be used as they tend to perish during prolonged storage. The metal clips expand slightly as they are heated so these jars are sealed before processing.

Saucepan and Stand

The preserves may be processed in the oven or in a saucepan. The saucepan must be deep enough to submerge the jars or bottles in water. The bottles must be placed on a stand in the base of the saucepan. Slats of wood or a thick pad of newspaper may be used as a stand for the jars.

Oven Method

If the preserve is processed in the oven, the jars are placed on a pad of paper in a roasting tin.

Tongs, Thermometer, Oven Glove and Wooden Board

Special preserving tongs are best for lifting hot jars. A thermometer should be used to check the temperature of water. An oven glove is essential for holding jars and a clean, dry wooden board must be used as a stand for hot jars. Jars placed on a cold or damp surface are liable to crack.

PREPARING THE JARS

The jars must be spotlessly clean. They should be washed in hot, soapy water, rinsed in boiling water and allowed to drain upside down on clean tea-towels. The jars should be left upside down to drain until they are filled.

If the jars have been stored for some time or are dirty, they should be sterilized. To sterilize jars, first wash them in hot, soapy water, rinse them, then stand them on slats of wood, a rack or a pad of paper in a deep pan. Pour in cold water to completely cover the jars. Put any lids, clips and rings into the pan. Heat gently until the water boils, then boil the jars for 5 minutes. Turn the heat off and leave the jars submerged until they are to be used, when they should be drained upside down on clean tea-towels spread on a work surface.

LIQUID FOR BOTTLING

Fruit is usually bottled in syrup; however, fruit juice may be used instead. The syrup may be combined with brandy or other spirits or liqueurs, or it may be flavoured with spices, such as cinnamon sticks or cloves. Strips of orange or lemon rind may also be used to flavour the syrup.

Syrup
There is no rule about the quantity of sugar used in a syrup for bottling. Heavy syrups tend to make the fruit rise in the jar which spoils the appearance of the preserve (only a problem if the bottled fruit is prepared for a competition or exhibition). Brown sugar may be used if preferred but the fruit will take on the dark colour. Honey may also be used to sweeten the bottling liquid. The following is a guide to the quantities of sugar to add to a litre / 1¾ pints of water when making syrup:

Light syrup – 200g / 7oz (for apples)
Medium syrup – 400–575g / 14oz–1½lb (for all fruit)
Heavy syrup – 800g / 1¾lb (for peaches)

Dissolve the sugar in the water, bring to the boil and boil for 2 minutes. Remove from the heat and cover the pan to prevent any extra water from evaporating.

PREPARING THE FRUIT

Only bottle perfectly fresh, prime-quality fruit. Wash, dry and trim the fruit, then cut it into even-sized pieces if necessary. Avoid overhandling the fruit. Soft fruits, in particular, should be handled as little as possible to avoid bruising or spoiling them. Scald a wooden spoon and use its handle to ease the fruit into position when packing the jars. The fruit should be closely packed but not squashed. Apples may be solidly packed, leaving little airspace or room for syrup.

Apples
Peel, core and cut into 5mm / ¼ inch thick slices or rings. Put into acidulated water (that is, water into which half a lemon has been squeezed) until all the apples are prepared to prevent discolouration. Drain well, then dry before packing. For solid packs, blanch apples in boiling water for 2 minutes, drain and pack.

Apricots
Ripe, not soft, apricots may be bottled whole or halved with stones removed. Crack some stones and add a few kernels to jars of halved fruit.

Blackberries
Select large, fully ripe fruit.

Cherries
Select plump fruit with small stones. Morello cherries are best. Remove stalks. Stone fruit if liked, reserving all juice to add to syrup.

Currants (black, red or white)
Select large, ripe fruit. String and pack. Redcurrants and whitecurrants have large seeds and are best mixed with raspberries.

Damsons
Remove stalks. Wipe to remove bloom. Pack whole.

Gooseberries
Select green, hard and unripe fruit. Top and tail, then cut off a small slice at each end if preserving in syrup to prevent skins from shriveling. Use a stainless steel knife to cut the fruit.

Loganberries

Select firm, deep red fruit, remove stalks and discard fruit attacked by maggots.

Mulberries

Bottle freshly picked fruit that is not overripe.

Peaches or Nectarines

A free-stone variety is best so that stones may be removed easily. Pour freshly boiled water over fruit, or plunge the fruit into a pan of boiling water, and leave for 30–60 seconds. Drain and skin. Halve the peaches and remove their stones. Work quickly, as peaches discolour on standing.

Pears – cooking

Firm cooking pears should be prepared as for dessert pears, then poached in medium syrup until tender. Use the cooking syrup for packing the fruit.

Pears – dessert

Select fruit that is just ripe. Peel, halve and core. Submerge prepared fruit in acidulated water (water with lemon juice) or lemon juice until ready to pack. Drain or rinse before packing if the lemon juice is not required.

Pineapple

Trim, peel and core. Remove all the eyes and cut the fruit into rings or cubes.

Plums

Select Victoria plums that are fully grown, firm and just turning pink. Select purple varieties that are still bright red. Yellow plums should be firm and lemon-yellow in colour. Trim and wipe to remove bloom. Free-stone varieties may be halved and stoned, others should be left whole.

Raspberries

Fruit must not be overripe. Pack freshly picked raspberries and avoid squashing.

Rhubarb

Select tender young rhubarb. Cut it into short lengths and pack. For a tight pack (not quite a solid pack), soak the prepared rhubarb in medium syrup for 8–12 hours. The rhubarb shrinks during soaking. When hard water is used for bottling rhubarb, a harmless white deposit collects on top of the liquid. Use boiled or softened water to avoid this.

Strawberries

Hull the fruit, which must not be overripe. Soak prepared strawberries in syrup as for rhubarb to shrink them before bottling.

PROCESSING METHODS

Follow these instructions very closely. When packing different fruits together, follow the highest temperature and longest processing time suggested for the types of fruit used.

QUICK PAN DEEP METHOD

1 Prepare the syrup or bottling liquid and the fruit. Pack the fruit into prepared jars and heat the syrup or bottling liquid to 60°C / 140°F.

2 Have ready a saucepan deep enough to submerge the jars. Place a rack, wooden slats or a thick pad of newspaper in the bottom of the pan, then half fill it with water. Heat the water to 38°C / 100°F.

3 Check the temperature of the syrup or packing liquid, making sure it is still 60°C / 140°F, then pour it into the jars. Dislodge any air bubbles from between the pieces of fruit by gently shaking the jars. The jars should be just overflowing with liquid.

4 Dip rubber rings (if used) in boiling water and put them on the jars. Fix the lids with metal clips. Put on screw bands, tighten them, then undo them by a quarter turn to allow room for the jar to expand as it is heated.

5 Stand the jars in the saucepan and make sure that they are submerged in the water. The jars must not touch each other or the side of the pan.

6 Cover the pan and bring to 90°C / 194°F in 20–25 minutes. Simmer for time indicated opposite. Using wooden tongs, transfer jars to a wooden surface. Tighten screw bands, if used. Clips should hold properly without attention. Leave for 24 hours.

7 Test the seal on each jar by removing the screw bands or clips and lifting the jars by their lids. If the lids stay firm they are properly sealed. Label and store.

PROCESSING TIMES FOR QUICK DEEP PAN METHOD

The following times are for jars with a maximum capacity of 1 litre / 1¼ pints:

- **2 minutes:** apple rings, blackberries, currants, gooseberries (for cooked puddings), loganberries, mulberries, raspberries, rhubarb (for cooked puddings), damsons and strawberries

- **10 minutes:** apricots, cherries, gooseberries (for cold desserts), whole plums, greengages, rhubarb (for cold desserts) and solid packs of soft fruit (excluding strawberries)

- **20 minutes:** solid pack apples, nectarines, peaches, pineapples, halved plums and solid pack strawberries

- **40 minutes:** whole tomatoes, pears

- **50 minutes:** tomatoes (in own juice)

MODERATE OVEN METHOD

The traditional oven method processes the fruit in the oven before adding the syrup; however, the fruit tends to shrink when processed without the syrup. The following method heats the fruit in the syrup to keep shrinkage to a minimum.

1 Heat the oven to 150°C / 300°F / gas 2. Fill warmed jars with prepared fruit.

2 Pour in boiling syrup or the chosen liquid to within 2 cm / ¾ inch of the top of each jar.

3 Dip rubber rings (if used) and lids in boiling water and fit them on the jars. Do not fit clips and screw bands.

4 Line a roasting tin with three or four layers of newspaper. Stand the jars 5 cm / 2 inches apart on the paper.

5 Put the jars in the middle of the oven and process for the times given in the table on the right.

6 Prepare a clean, dry wooden surface on which to stand the jars. Immediately check that the necks of the jars are clean, wiping them with absorbent kitchen paper, and fit the screw bands or clips.
WARNING: Do not wipe the jars with a damp cloth or they will crack.

7 Leave for 24 hours before testing the seal by removing the screw bands or clips and lifting the jars by their lids. If the lids stay firm they are properly sealed. Label and store.

PROCESSING TIMES FOR MODERATE OVEN METHOD

Note: 4 x 350ml / 12 fl oz jars require the same processing time as 2 x 700ml / 1 pint 3¼ fl oz jars.

- **30–40 minutes (up to 2kg / 4½lb) or 50–60 minutes (2–4.5kg / 4½–10lb):** apple rings, blackberries, currants, gooseberries (for cooked puddings), loganberries, mulberries, raspberries and rhubarb

- **40–50 minutes (up to 2kg / 4½lb) or 55—70 minutes (2–4.5kg / 4½–10lb):** apricots, cherries, damsons, gooseberries (for cold desserts), whole plums and rhubarb (for cold desserts)

- **50–60 minutes (up to 2kg / 4½lb) or 65–80 minutes (2–4.5kg / 4½–10lb):** solid pack apples, nectarines, peaches, pineapple and halved plums

- **60–70 minutes (up to 2kg / 4½lb) or 75—90 minutes (2–4.5kg / 4½–10lb):** pears

STORING BOTTLED FRUIT

Store the sealed jars or bottles in a cool, dark, dry cupboard.

APPLES
PRESERVED IN QUARTERS

3.6kg / 8lb apples
2.7kg / 6lb sugar
3.4 litres / 6 pints water
juice 4 lemons

Peel, quarter and core the apples. Place the apple peeling and cores in the water, add the sugar, simmer gently for about 25 minutes, and strain until clear. Replace the syrup in the pan, add the apples and lemon juice, and simmer gently until the apples are tender, but not broken. Place them in jars or wide necked bottles, pour the syrup over them, and cover so as completely to exclude the air. Store in a cool, dry place.

APRICOTS
BOTTLED

Choose some firm, yellow apricots – not too ripe. Cut them in half, and take out the stones. Blanch them in boiling water until tender, then drop them into cold water. Next peel them, and put them in bottles. Break the stones and extract the kernels, blanch and add a few of the kernels. Then fill the bottles three quarters full with syrup, seal, and finish as for Cherries, Bottled (page 70).

APRICOTS
PRESERVED

Choose some fine, yellow apricots – not too ripe – run the point of a small knife into the fruit near the stalk, and work it slightly round the stone, which can then be gently squeezed out. Blanch the apricots in boiling water until tender when they will rise to the surface, then drop them into cold water. Prepare a syrup and boil it to the 'large blow' (111°C / 233°F). Put in the apricots and boil up twice, then withdraw from the heat, remove the scum, and finish as with Greengages, Preserved (page 75).

BARBERRIES
PRESERVED IN BUNCHES

Prepare some small pieces of clean white wood 7.5 cm / 3 inches long and 5mm / ¼ inch wide; tie the fruit to these in nice bunches. Have ready some clear syrup; put in the barberries, and simmer them in it for about half an hour on two successive days, and covering them each time with syrup when cold. When the fruit looks perfectly clear it is sufficiently done, and should be stored away in pots, with the syrup poured over.

CHERRIES, RED
BOTTLED

Procure some fine Kentish cherries, cut off the stalks, and put them in bottles. Choose wide-mouthed bottles, and see that they are perfectly clean and dry. Next prepare a syrup. Take 450g / 1lb granulated sugar, dissolve it in 1 litre / 2 pints water, and fill the bottles about three quarters up with it, then seal. Place the bottles upright in a copper or large saucepan, with cold water up to their necks, and gradually heat them to the first boiling. Withdraw from the heat, and let the fruit stand in the copper till next day. Then take the bottles out, clean them, cover, pack with the mouths downwards and store in a dry place.

CHERRIES, UNSWEETENED
BOTTLED

Procure some Kentish cherries, stone them, and put them into bottles. Seal them, and gradually heat up to about 93°C / 200°F. Withdraw from the heat, and finish in the same way as with other bottled fruits.

CHERRIES
PRESERVED

**To each 450g / 1lb sound, ripe cooking cherries allow
225g / ½lb preserving sugar and 150ml / ¼ pint water**

Remove the stones carefully, keeping the fruit as whole as possible. Boil the sugar and water to a syrup, add the cherries, simmer them gently for about 15 minutes, then turn both fruit and syrup into a large basin, and put aside until the following day. Strain the syrup into a preserving-pan; to each 600ml / 1 pint add from 100–175g / 4–6oz of sugar, according to taste, bring to boiling-point, skim well, then put in the fruit and simmer gently for about 10 minutes. Pour into jars, cover and store in a cool, dry place.

Note: The flavour may be considerably improved by substituting the juice of either red or white currants for the water.

CHERRIES, RED
PRESERVED OR CRYSTALLIZED

Procure some fine Kentish cherries, stone them, and put them into a pan with sufficient boiling syrup to cover them. Boil up three or four times, withdraw from the heat, remove the scum, and finish as for Greengages, Preserved (page 75).

CURRANTS
BOTTLED

Choose some fine currants, pick them over, and put them in bottles. Seal and proceed as for unsweetened cherries.

DAMSONS
BOTTLED

Remove the stalks but not the stones, place the fruit in wide-necked glass bottles, and tie a piece of waxed paper securely over the top of each one. Cover the bottom of a large boiling pot with a thin layer of newspaper, stand the bottles side by side on the top of it, and surround them with cold water. Bring slowly to boiling point, then remove the boiling pot from the heat, but let the bottles remain in it until the contents are perfectly cold. Before storing them remove the waxed paper, fill the mouths of the bottles with sugar, and seal tightly. Store in a cool, dry place.

DAMSONS (OR PLUMS)
BOTTLED (WITHOUT SUGAR)

Let the fruit be dry and sound. Place it in wide-necked jars, cover completely with boiling water, and cover to exclude the air completely. The fruit will keep a considerable time, and when required for use the water should be poured off, and the jelly at the bottom of the jar used to improve the flavour of the fruit.

DAMSONS
BAKED, FOR KEEPING

Fruit for preserving in this manner should be perfectly sound, and not over-ripe. Remove the stalks, but not the stones. To each 450g / 1lb of fruit allow 225g / ½lb of sugar. Place the fruit and sugar in a large casserole dish in alternate layers, cover closely, and bake in a very cool oven until the plums are tender. Pack the plums closely in large jars, pour the syrup over, and when quite cold cover securely. If stored in a cool, dry place, the fruit will keep good for 3 or 4 months.

FIGS
PRESERVED

**To each 450g / 1lb green figs allow 450g / 1lb sugar
and 300ml / ½ pint water**

Make a slit across the top of each fig, cover them with brine that will float an egg, and let them remain for 8 days. Drain well, boil gently in a little water until quite tender, then drain again and cover with cold water. Change the water daily for 3 days, and on the third day have ready a syrup made of the sugar and water in the proportions given above. Boil the figs in the syrup for about 10 minutes, repeat the process daily for 3 or 4 days, until the figs are tender and green. Place them in jars or bottles, add the syrup, cover closely, and store in a dry, cool place.

FRUIT, FRESH
BOTTLED (WITH SUGAR)

Allow 100g / 4oz of preserving sugar to each 2 pints of fruit, and follow the directions given under Gooseberries, Bottled (with sugar) (page 74).

GOOSEBERRIES
BOTTLED (WITHOUT SUGAR)

Use firm, sound unripe green gooseberries

Head and tail the gooseberries, put into wide necked glass bottles, cover with water and secure the lids. Wrap a little newspaper round each bottle. Put a thin layer of paper on the bottom of a large pan, stand the bottles on top and add enough cold water to come at least three-quarters up the sides. Bring the water slowly to boiling point, then remove the pan from the heat, but allow the bottles to remain in it until the gooseberries begin to rise in them. Now add a little boiling water to each and seal. Place them on their sides in a cool, dry place.

GOOSEBERRIES
BOTTLED (WITH SUGAR)

To each 450g / 1lb firm, sound, green gooseberries
allow 450g / 1lb granulated sugar
and 300ml / ½ pint water

Head and tail the gooseberries, cover them with cold water simmer slowly until tender, but unbroken, then drain well and put them into cold water. Dissolve the sugar in the water, boil to a syrup, then let it become quite cold. Drain the gooseberries well, put them into the cold syrup, bring to boiling-point, boil gently for 10 minutes, then turn the whole into a bowl. Next day drain the syrup into a preserving-pan, boil it to the 'large thread' degree (103°C / 217°F), then put in the fruit and boil gently for about 10 minutes. Turn into hot, dry, bottles and seal securely.

GOOSEBERRIES, GREEN
PRESERVED

Choose some fine large gooseberries – not too ripe – pick them and blanch them, add a little soda or salt to keep them green, and finish as for Greengages, Preserved (page 75).

GREENGAGES
BOTTLED

Proceed as for Apricots, Bottled (page 69).

GREENGAGES
PRESERVED

Choose some good greengages, take a fine skewer or large needle and prick them all over, then drop them into a pan of cold water. Place the pan on the heat, blanch the fruit, and remove the pan when just at boiling-point. Take out the greengages with a skimmer when they float on the surface of the water, and drop them into cold water. Drain them on a sieve.

Then prepare a plain syrup, boil it to the 'small thread' (101°C / 215°F), add the greengages, and let them gently boil. Withdraw from the heat and remove the scum, pour them into a pan, and next day drain the syrup off. Add more sugar, and boil up again to the 'large thread' (102°C / 217°F). Repeat this process for 6 days, the last time boiling the sugar to the 'large pearl' (105°C / 222°F).

Note: Soft fruits should not be boiled in the syrup, but require the boiling syrup to be poured on them. Preserved fruits should be kept in a dry place – not too warm, as heat causes fermentation, and damp makes them mouldy.

GREENGAGES
PRESERVED IN SYRUP

**To each 450g / 1lb greengages allow 450g / 1lb preserving sugar
and 150ml / ¼ pint water**

Proceed exactly as in the recipe for Greengage Jam I (page 23), with the exception of removing the stones before putting the fruit into the syrup. Boil the fruit for about 10 minutes on 3 consecutive days, adding on the last day half the kernels, which should be previously blanched. Throughout the whole process the scum must be carefully removed as it rises, otherwise the syrup will not be clear.

GREEN GINGER
PRESERVED

Put the ginger regularly every night and morning for a fortnight into fresh boiling water. Remove the outside skin with a sharp knife, boil it in water until it is quite soft, and slice it in thin slices. Make ready a syrup of 450g / 1lb of granulated sugar to 300ml / ½ pint of water, clarify it, and put the ginger into it. Boil until it is clear.

LEMONS, FANCY

Prepare in the same way as for Fancy Oranges (page 77).

MANGOES
PRESERVED

Let the mangoes lie for a few hours in cold water, then peel them thinly and remove the stones. Cover with water with a dash of lime juice, and at the end of 1 hour drain well and place them in a preserving-pan. Barely cover with cold water, boil gently for about 10 minutes, and drain well. Replace the mangoes in the pan, cover with sugar syrup, boil gently until the sugar begins to crystallize, and, when cool, transfer carefully into jars or wide-necked bottles. During the first month the syrup must be examined from time to time, and if it appears at all thin it should be re-boiled. It may be necessary to repeat this process two or three times before finally sealing and storing.

MIRABELLE PLUMS
BOTTLED

Choose some fine Mirabelle plums – not too ripe. Prick them, and drop them into boiling water for a few minutes; then take them out with a skimmer, and drop them into cold water. Strain, and put them into bottles, add the syrup, and finish as for other fruits.

NECTARINES
PRESERVED

ripe nectarines
preserving sugar

Put half the fruit into a jar, cover closely, place it on the stove in a large saucepan of cold water, and cook slowly until the juice is extracted. Strain, measure the juice, and put it into a preserving-pan with the addition of 900g / 2lb of sugar to each 600ml / 1 pint of juice. Bring to boiling point, skim well, add the remainder of the fruit, and boil until it is half-cooked. Turn the whole into a bowl, unless the preserving-pan is lined with enamel, in which case they may remain in the pan. On the following day boil until the juice sets quickly when tested on a cold plate. Turn into pots, cover closely, and store in a cool, dry place.

ORANGES, FANCY

Choose some round, smooth oranges, cut on the rind any fancy designs, such as stars, circles, etc. When the oranges are decorated, blanch them in boiling water until tender, and then drop them into cold water. Boil a plain syrup to the 'small thread' (102°C / 215°F). Drain and dry the oranges, then drop them into the syrup. Boil up two or three times, removing the scum. Then finish as for other fruits.

ORANGES AND LEMONS
PRESERVED WHOLE

**To each 450g / 1lb oranges allow 900g / 2lb sugar
and 600ml / 1 pint water;
to lemons allow 1.4kg / 3lb sugar and 900ml / 1½ pints water**

At one end of each orange make a hole sufficiently large to admit a small spoon, and scoop out the pulp and juice. Place them in a preserving-pan with sufficient cold water to cover them, simmer gently until tender, and drain well. Boil the sugar and water to a syrup, add the juice and pulp, boil gently for about 15 minutes, and pour the whole over the oranges. When quite cold, replace in the pan, simmer very gently for about half an hour, then turn into a bowl. On the following day boil up the syrup and pour it over the oranges; this process should be repeated on two or three consecutive days until the rinds are quite clear. Fill the oranges with syrup, place them in wide-necked jars, pour the remainder of the syrup over them, and cover closely. Store in a cool, dry place.

PEARS
BOTTLED

Only firm, mature fruit should be selected for bottling. Wipe them clean, pare thinly, cut into quarters and core. Pack the fruit as tightly as possible into the bottles or jars. Fill to the brim with water, fit on the lid or screw cap and sterilize in the usual manner. They should be kept at boiling point for 15 minutes.

PEARS
PRESERVED

3.6kg / 8lb firm, sound pears
2.7kg / 6lb preserving sugar
finely grated rind and juice 3 lemons
5-cm / 2-inch piece ginger

Select a pan with a close fitting lid, cover the bottom to the depth of 2.5cm / 1 inch with cold water, put in the fruit and sugar in layers, and add the ginger, lemon rind and lemon juice. Cover closely, place the pan over a saucepan of boiling water, and cook slowly until the pears are quite tender but not broken. Put them carefully into jars, strain the syrup over them, and cover. The pears will keep good for 3 or 4 months if stored in a cool, dry place.

PEARS, RED
PRESERVED

Proceed as for White Pears, below. Add sufficient cochineal to give the pears a delicate, but not too deep a tint of red.

PEARS, WHITE
PRESERVED

Choose some fine large pears – not too ripe – prick them over, and blanch them until a pin's head runs easily through them. Drop them into cold water, pare off the rind very thinly, and prick them again to the core. Drop them into another pan of cold water, drain them, and put them into a thin syrup boiled to the 'Small Thread' (102°C / 215°F). Remove the scum, and finish as for Greengages, Preserved (page 75).

PEARS AND CHERRIES
IN WHITE PORT

600ml / 1 pint white port
900g / 2lb sugar
600ml / 1 pint water
piece cinnamon stick
450g / 1lb Morello cherries
1.8kg / 4lb pears, peeled, cored and halved
a little yellow or orange food colouring (optional)

Put the port, sugar, water and cinnamon stick into a saucepan and bring to the boil. Add the cherries (unstoned) and simmer until the syrup is thick and the cherries are almost tender.

Add the pear halves and bring the syrup to the boil once more. Simmer for 2–3 minutes, but do not allow the pears to soften. Stir in the colouring and pour immediately into sterilized jars, until the syrup is about to overflow, and seal.

PINEAPPLE I
PRESERVED

Choose 1 or 2 fine pineapples, cut off the top and the stalk and pare the rind outside the pine. Then prick to the core with a large needle in several places. Place the pine in a pan with plenty of water, boil until tender, and finish the preparation as for Apricots, Preserved (page 69).

PINEAPPLE II
PRESERVED

Cut the pineapples into slices 5mm / ¼ inch in thickness, trim off the edges, and remove the hard centre part. Put these trimmings into a preserving-pan with sufficient water to cover them, and simmer them gently for about half an hour. Strain, return to the pan, add the sliced pineapples, caster or granulated sugar to taste, and simmer gently for about half an hour, skimming occasionally meanwhile. Pineapples thus preserved will not keep long.

MRS BEETON'S TIP

It isn't always easy to tell whether a pineapple is ripe or not. A delicious aroma is a good guide, as is a dull solid sound when the side of the fruit is tapped with a finger. Good quality pineapples generally have small, compact crowns. Green fruit are not ripe.

PLUMS
PRESERVED

**To each 450g / 1lb plums allow 450g / 1lb granulated sugar
and 300ml / ½ pint water**

Put the water and sugar into a preserving-pan and boil to a thin syrup.
Remove the stalks from the plums, prick them slightly to prevent them breaking, pour over them the prepared syrup, and allow them to remain thus for
2 days. Turn the whole into a preserving-pan, boil very gently until the plums
are tender, then lift them carefully into pots. Boil the syrup to the 'Large
Thread' degree (102°C / 217°F), pour it over the plums, cover closely, and
store in a cool, dry place.

PUMPKIN
PRESERVED

**To each 450g / 1lb pumpkin allow 450g / 1lb preserving sugar,
2 tbsp lemon juice, finely grated rind of 1 lemon
and 2.5ml / ½ tsp ground ginger**

Pare and halve the pumpkin, remove the seeds, and slice thinly. Lay the slices
on a large dish, covering each layer thickly with sugar, add the lemon-juice, and
leave covered for 1 day. Turn the whole into a preserving-pan, add the lemon
rind and ginger, and 300ml / ½ pint of cold water to 1.4kg / 3lb of fruit, bring
slowly to boiling point, and continue the cooking until the slices of pumpkin are
quite tender, but not broken. Lift the slices of pumpkin carefully into jars, and
strain the syrup into a preserving-pan. Boil the syrup to the 'Large Pearl' stage
(105°C / 222°F), pour it over the pumpkin, cover closely, and when cold, put the
jars into a cool, dry place.

QUINCES
PRESERVED

Pare, quarter, core the quinces, and preserve the skins and cores. Put the fruit into the preserving-pan with barely enough water to cover them, and simmer until soft, but not broken. Place the quinces singly on large dishes, add the cores and parings to the water in which the quinces were cooked, and simmer gently for about 1 hour. Strain through a jelly-bag until quite clear, return it to the pan with the addition of 450g / 1lb of sugar for each 450g / 1lb of fruit, bring to boiling point, and skim well. Put in the quinces, boil for about 15 minutes, then turn the whole carefully into an earthenware bowl, and let the preparation remain until the following day. Drain the syrup once more into the pan; when boiling add the fruit, cook gently for 15 minutes or so, then lift the quinces carefully into small jars, which they should three quarters fill. Continue boiling the syrup until it forms a thick jelly when tested on a cold plate, pour it over the fruit, cover the jars closely and store in a cool, dry place.

RASPBERRIES
BOTTLED

Proceed as for Gooseberries, Bottled (page 73).

STRAWBERRIES, etc
BOTTLED

For each of these preserves proceed in the same way as for all other fruits of this kind, taking care that the fruit, in each case, is sound, and not too ripe.

STRAWBERRIES I
PRESERVED

equal weight of strawberries and granulated sugar

Strawberries for preserving must be very dry, otherwise they will not keep; the stalks must be removed, and any unsound fruit rejected.

Put the sugar into a preserving-pan; to each 450g / 1lb add 300ml / ½ pint of cold water and a small pinch of cream of tartar, and boil to the 'Small Ball' degree (114°C / 237°F). Now put in the prepared fruit, cover the pan, allow it to remain on the stove, but on the lowest possible heat, for about 1 hour, then bring the contents to boiling-point and skim well. Boil gently for a few minutes, then turn into jars, cover closely, and store in a cool, dry place.

STRAWBERRIES II
PRESERVED

**To each 450g / 1lb strawberries allow 450g / 1lb preserving sugar
and 150ml / ¼ pint redcurrant juice
*(See Redcurrant Jelly, page 60)***

Pick over the strawberries, pile them on a large dish, sprinkle with half the sugar, and let them remain thus until the following day. Prepare the redcurrant juice as directed, pour into a preserving-pan with the remaining sugar, and boil to a thin syrup. Turn the fruit and syrup into the juice and boil gently until the syrup sets quickly when tested on a cold plate. Pour gently into pots and keep in a cool, dry place.

Fruits in Brandy

*These indulgent preserves make excellent gifts.
Try them with cream or ice-cream for
dessert, or use them as the basis
of a boozy fruit crumble.*

The preparation of fruit in brandy is exactly the same as for preserved fruits. All fruits containing pectin or vegetable jelly, such as apricots, red cherries, greengages, peaches, etc, may be preserved in brandy. Care should be taken to select suitable fruits, viz, those which are firm, and not too ripe. Fruits that are too ripe will not keep, and soon become mashed to a marmalade in the bottles.

APRICOTS IN BRANDY

Take some fine yellow apricots – not too ripe – prick them over, then blanch them in boiling water until they are soft but not too tender. When the apricots rise to the surface, drop them in cold water, drain them on a sieve, and prepare a plain syrup. Put in the apricots and let them boil, remove from the heat, and mix to every pint of syrup 1 litres / 2 pints of best brandy. Put the apricots into clean, dry bottles, and pour over the liquor. When cold, make the bottles airtight.

BLACKCURRANTS IN BRANDY

Take some fine blackcurrants, prick, and wash them in cold water. Drain them on a sieve. Have ready some cherry brandy, and add the blackcurrants. Boil gently for a few minutes, remove from the heat and bottle when cold.

CHERRIES IN BRANDY

Take some fine morello cherries. Remove the stems, then drop them into cold water. Wash them well, drain them on a sieve, and put them into clean, dry bottles. Next pour over sufficient brandy to cover them, add a little cinnamon, make the bottles airtight, and allow them to remain for a month. Then drain off the brandy, and to each 600ml / 1 pint add 100g / 4oz of caster sugar. Mix well and melt it, then strain the liquor until it is bright and clear, and pour this over the cherries. They are then ready for use.

GREENGAGES
IN BRANDY

Take some fine greengages – not too ripe – prick them with a fork, put them into a pan of water with a little alum in it, and set the pan over the heat. When tender, put them into cold water and let them stand for 2 hours. Prepare a plain syrup, and finish as for Apricots in Brandy (page 86).

MIRABELLE PLUMS
IN BRANDY

Prepare in the same way as Apricots in Brandy (page 86).

ORANGES IN BRANDY

Choose some fine large oranges, put them into a pan of hot water, and boil until tender. Then drop them into cold water, and drain them. Prepare a plain syrup. Put the oranges in it, and let them boil for about 5 minutes. Remove from the heat, and finish as for Apricots in Brandy (page 86).

PEACHES IN BRANDY I

Proceed as for Apricots in Brandy (page 86), taking care not to bruise or crush the fruit.

PEACHES IN BRANDY II

2.7kg / 6 lb peaches
1.4kg / 3 lb caster or powdered granulated sugar
1.7 litres / 3 pints brandy

Peaches intended for preserving should be firm, sound, and not over-ripe.

Remove the stones, taking care to keep the fruit as whole as possible, place the fruit in a large pan, and cover each layer thickly with sugar. Add the brandy, cover closely, place the pan over a saucepan of boiling water, and heat gently until the brandy is on the point of boiling. Remove the fruit carefully to hot, dry, small pots, add to each an equal share of the hot brandy, and cover closely. Store in a cool, dry place.

PEARS IN BRANDY

Take some fine large eating pears – not too ripe or juicy – prick them all over, blanch them until soft, and then drop them into cold water. Pare off the rind very thinly, prick the pears well with a fine skewer or large needle, and drop them into another pan of cold water. Put the pan on the heat again until the fruit is thoroughly scalded, or blanched, and can easily be run through with a fine skewer or large needle. Put them again into cold water, drain, and finish as for Apricots in Brandy (page 86).

Fruit Pastes & Candies

Fruit pastes can be dried or stored as pulp, and have a wide variety of uses as snacks, accompaniments and decorations. This chapter also includes candied fruits.

CANDIED AND CRYSTALLIZED FRUITS

With good basic equipment, plenty of time, patience and enthusiasm, skills such as working with sugar can readily be mastered.

EQUIPMENT

A stainless steel or other high-quality saucepan and sugar thermometer are the first items you need. A marble board and large palette knife are best for working boiled sugar syrup, although a plain white (fairly heavy) enamelled tray may be used instead. Some work surfaces withstand the heat of the boiled sugar: others do not. Marble gives the best results.

Chocolate Work

Depending on the type of chocolates you hope to make, you may need moulds and / or a dipping fork (a fine, two-pronged fork). To pipe detail on the set chocolates you will need small greaseproof paper piping bags and a small, plain piping tube (from suppliers of cake decorating materials).

SUGAR BOILING

Refer to pages 8–9 for the degrees of sugar and simple tests to gauge the desired consistency.

A LOAF OF SUGAR

When sugar first arrived in Britain with other spices from the Orient in the thirteenth century, it was shaped into flat blocks called sugar cakes. These had to be crushed before the sugar could be used. A process for refining and crystallizing sugar into conical loaves was invented in Venice in the late fifteenth century and this method continued until the late 1800s. The loaves weighed anything between 2.25kg / 5lb and 16kg / 35lb and were broken into convenient pieces with special choppers and strong iron nippers. Until a high tax was reduced in 1874, sugar was very expensive and poor people had to use low quality, coarse sugar that did not make very good jam.

THE PROCESS

Shop-bought candied fruit is a succulent and expensive luxury but it can be made at home without great skill or special equipment. The main requirement is patience as the process takes about 15 minutes a day for 10–14 days. Any attempt to increase the strength of the syrup too quickly will result in tough, hardened, and shrivelled fruit. Sugar alone can be used for syrup making but the fruit's texture is better if part of the sugar is replaced by glucose. Powdered glucose weighs the same as sugar, but if using liquid glucose, increase the weight by one-fifth.

Use well-flavoured fruits, fresh or canned, for example apricots, pineapple or large, juicy plums. Very soft fruits, such as raspberries, tend to disintegrate. Fresh fruit should be firm yet ripe. Good quality canned fruit can be used; it lacks some of the full fresh flavour, but the canning process gives a good texture for candying. Canned fruit does not require cooking and the process is quicker than for fresh fruit.

Processed fruit should be packed in waxed-paper lined cardboard boxes. Interleave layers of fruit with waxed paper. Store in a cool, dry place: well-processed fruit will keep for several months.

FRESH FRUIT

Day 1: Prepare the fruit according to type, discarding stones and cores or peel. Prick small crab-apples, apricots, fleshy plums or greengages several times to the centre with a stainless steel fork.

Cover the prepared fruit with boiling water and simmer gently until just tender, 10–15 minutes for firm fruits, only 3–4 minutes for tender fruits. Overcooking at this stage makes the fruit squashy, while undercooking makes it dark and tough.

For each 450g / 1lb fruit, make a syrup from 250ml / 8 fl oz poaching water, 50g / 2oz sugar and 100g / 4oz glucose. Alternatively, use 150g / 5oz preserving sugar instead of sugar and glucose. Stir until the sugar has dissolved, then bring it to the boil.

Drain the fruit and place it in a small bowl, then pour the boiling syrup over it. If there is not enough syrup to cover it, make up some more, using the same proportions. Cover with a plate to keep the fruit under the syrup and leave for 24 hours.

Day 2: Drain the syrup into a saucepan. Add 50g / 2oz sugar for each original 250ml / 8 fl oz water. Bring to the boil, then pour the syrup over the fruit. Cover and leave as before.

Days 3–7: Repeat Day 2.

Day 8: Add 75g / 3oz sugar for every original 250ml / 8 fl oz water, heat and stir until dissolved. Add the drained fruit and boil for 3–4 minutes, then pour fruit and syrup back into the bowl. This boiling makes the fruit plump. Leave for 48 hours.

Day 10: Repeat Day 8. When cooled, the resulting syrup should be of the consistency of fairly thick honey. If the syrup is still thin, repeat day 8 again. Leave for 4 days.

Day 14: The fruit will keep in this heavy syrup for 2–3 weeks or for 2 months in a covered jar in the refrigerator. To complete the process, remove the fruit from the syrup.

WARNING: Do not pierce the fruit. Place it on a wire rack over a plate and allow to drain for a few minutes.

Put the rack into a very cool oven (not higher than 50°C / 122°F). Use an oven thermometer to check the temperature and wedge the door ajar to prevent the temperature from increasing.

Candied fruit caramelizes easily and the flavour is then spoiled. Drying should take 3–6 hours if the heat is continuous; it may take 2–3 days if using residual heat on several occasions. Do not allow the metal rack to touch the hot sides of the oven as this will cause the wire to become too hot. Turn the fruit gently with a fork, until it is no longer sticky to handle.

Pack in cardboard boxes with waxed paper lining the box and separating the layers. Store in a dry, cool place and do not keep for many months as the succulence will be lost.

Candied fruit should have a dry surface. If it remains sticky, the final sugar concentration in the fruit is probably too low. Humid storage conditions should be avoided.

CANNED FRUITS

Try pineapple rings or cubes, plums, peaches or halved apricots. Keep the sizes as uniform as possible. These quantities are for about 450g / 1lb drained fruit.
Day 1: Put the drained fruit into a large bowl. Measure the syrup into a pan and make it up to 250ml / 8 fl oz with water if necessary. Add 200g / 7 oz sugar or 100g / 4oz glucose. Heat gently and stir until the sugar has dissolved. Bring to the boil, then pour the syrup over the fruit. If there is not enough syrup to cover the fruit, prepare some more by using 225g / 8oz sugar to 200ml / 7 fl oz water. Keep the fruit under the syrup with a plate. Leave for 24 hours.

Day 2: rain the fruit, dissolve 50g / 2oz sugar in the syrup, bring to the boil and pour over the fruit. Leave for 24 hours.

Days 3–4: Repeat Day 2.

Day 5: Pour the syrup into a saucepan. Add 75g / 3oz sugar, warm the syrup to dissolve the sugar, then add the fruit. Boil for 3–4 minutes. Replace in the bowl. Leave for 48 hours.

Day 7: Repeat Day 6 and let the fruit boil until a little syrup cooled on a plate has the consistency of thick honey. Leave to soak for 3–4 days. If the syrup seems thin, add a further 75g / 3oz sugar, dissolve it and boil the syrup with the fruit for a further few minutes. Leave to soak for 3–4 days.

Day 11: Finish the fruit as when candying fresh fruit (Day 14).

CANDIED ANGELICA

Pick bright, tender stalks in April, cut off the root ends and leaves. Make a brine with 15g / ½ oz salt in 2 litres / 3½ pints water, bring it to the boil. Soak the stalks in brine for 10 minutes. Rinse in cold water. Put in a pan of fresh boiling water and boil for 5–7 minutes. Drain. Scrape to remove the outer skin. Continue as for candying fresh fruit from Day 1 (page 91).

CANDIED PEEL

Use oranges, lemons or grapefruit. Scrub the fruit thoroughly. Halve and remove the pulp carefully to avoid damaging the peel, which is bitter, several changes of water. Drain, and continue as for candying fresh fruit from Day 1 (page 91). It is customary to pour some glacé syrup into half peels to set.

CRYSTALLIZING FRUIT

Before fruit can be subjected to the final process by which it is preserved for use in these two forms, it must first be boiled in syrup. The fruit to be candied or iced is dried before the fire or in a cool oven, the syrup in which it was cooked being meanwhile boiled to the 'large blow' degree ($111°C$ / $233°F$). When the syrup has cooled a little, the fruit should be dipped into it until thoroughly coated, and then dried, when they will have a transparent coating. Fruit to be crystallized should, immediately on its removal from the syrup, be rolled in crushed granulated sugar and afterwards dried.

Have some granulated sugar on a sheet of polythene, greaseproof paper or foil. Lift a piece of fruit on a fork, dip it quickly into boiling water, drain briefly, then roll it in the sugar until evenly coated.

MAKING A GLACÉ FINISH

This gives a smooth, shiny finish. Over gentle heat, dissolve 450g / 1lb granulated sugar in 150ml / ¼ pint water, the boil. Dip each fruit into boiling water for 20 seconds, then drain. Pour a little boiling syrup into a warm cup, quickly dip the fruit and place it on a wire rack. When all the fruit has been dipped, place the rack in a temperature not exceeding $50°C$ / $122°F$, and turn the fruit often to ensure even drying.

When the syrup in the small cup becomes cloudy, it must be discarded and replaced from the saucepan, which must be kept hot (but not boiling) and closely covered.

QUICK
CANDIED PEEL

Soak grapefuit or lemon peel overnight to extract some of the bitterness. Cut the peel into long strips, 5mm / ¼ inch wide. Put in a saucepan, cover with cold water and bring slowly to the boil. Drain, add fresh water and bring to the boil again. Drain, and repeat 3 more times. Weigh the cooled peel and place with an equal quantity of sugar in a pan. Just cover with boiling water, and boil gently until the peel is tender and clear. Cool, strain from the syrup, and toss the peel in fine granulated sugar on greaseproof paper. Spread out on a wire rack to dry for several hours. Roll again in sugar if at all sticky. When quite dry, store in covered jars. Use within 3–4 months.

MRS BEETON'S TIP

If you are candying several fruits at the same time, use separate syrups. Use surplus syrup for fruit salads, stewed fruits or sweetening puddings.

APPLE PASTE

Take 1.8kg / 4lb of apples, boil them in water until they are soft, then mash them, and pass them through a sieve into a pan. Next, boil 1.8kg / 4lb of granulated sugar to the 'Small Crack' (143°C / 290°F), remove from the heat, and pour the sugar into the pan with the mashed apples. Put the pan on the heat, and stir the contents well while boiling, until it comes away from the sides of the pan. Remove the mixture from the heat, and pour it out in a thin layer on baking trays powdered with sugar. Put the trays in an oven to dry until next day, then turn the paste over in order that it may dry both sides. When ready, take out and cut the paste into long, narrow strips. These can be shaped into knots or other form, such as rings, leaves, bon-bons, crosses, gimlets, sticks, lozenges, etc.

APRICOT PASTE

Take 900g / 2lb of apricots. Pass them through a fine sieve, add 450g / 1lb of sugar to 450g / 1lb of pulp, put them on a high heat, and stir well as they boil until the mixture leaves the bottom of the pan. Remove from the heat, and finish as for Apple Paste (above).

APRICOT PULP
PRESERVED

Take some fine ripe apricots, stone them, and pass them through a fine sieve into a basin. Weigh the pulp, adding to every 1.8kg / 4lb, 450g / 1lb of finely sifted caster sugar. Break the stones and take out the kernels. Blanch them, cut them in halves, and add some of them to the pulp. Put the pulp into clean, dry jars with lids, then place them upright in a pan with enough cold water to cover them. Put the pan on the heat and boil up well, then withdraw from the heat and let them stand until the next day. When quite cold, take out, and store in a dry place until required.

BLACKCURRANT PASTE

Pass the currants through a fine sieve. Put them into a pan and boil for about 15 minutes. Remove the pan from the heat, and weigh the pulp. Add 450g / 1lb of granulated sugar to each 450g / 1lb of pulp, mix well, and finish as for other pastes.

CHERRIES
DRIED

Cherries may be put into a slow oven and thoroughly dried before they begin to change colour. They should then be taken out of the oven, tied in bunches, and stored away in a dry place. In the winter they may be cooked with sugar for dessert. Particular care must be taken that the oven be not too hot. Another method of drying cherries is to stone them and put them into a preserving-pan with plenty of granulated sugar strewn among them. They should be simmered till the fruit shrivels, then they should be strained from the juice. The cherries should then be placed in an oven cool enough to dry without baking them. About 175g / 6oz of sugar will be required for 450g / 1lb of cherries, and the same syrup may be used again to do another quantity of fruit.

CHESTNUTS
CRYSTALLIZED

Choose some fine chestnuts. Take off the outside skin, and blanch them in sufficient boiling water until a needle runs through them easily. Then take off the inner or thin yellow skin, and drop them into warm water. Drain and put them into syrup, and let them simmer gently until the syrup becomes thick – the syrup should never be allowed to boil. Take out the chestnuts, and drain them on a sieve. Boil some syrup to the 'small blow' (110°C / 230°F) in a small pan, and just before it is quite cold work it against the side edges of the pan. Into this dip the chestnuts with a fork, place on trays, and dry them in a cool oven.

DAMSON CHEESE

Remove the stalks from the damsons, and put the fruit into a large casserole dish. Cover closely, cook in a very slow oven until perfectly soft, then rub through a fine sieve. Measure the pulp, and put it into a preserving-pan with the addition of 350–450g / 12–16oz of sugar to each 600ml / 1 pint of pulp, according to individual taste. Boil until the greater part of the syrup has evaporated and the pulp has become rather stiff, stirring frequently at first and almost continuously towards the end of the process. Turn into small jars, cover closely, and store in a cool, dry place. The stones may be cracked and the kernels added to the purée with the sugar.

MRS BEETON'S TIP

The fruit may be baked in a traditional ovenproof earthenware jar, is preferred. It will require 2–3 hours in a preheated 110°C / 225°F / gas ¼ oven.

DAMSON PASTE

Proceed exactly as in making Apricot Paste, page 97.

GREENGAGE PASTE

Greengage Paste is made in the same manner as Apricot Paste, page 97, both as regards the proportions of fruit, and sugar and the method of preparation.

GREENGAGES
PRESERVED DRY

**To each 450g / 1lb greengages allow 450g / 1lb sugar
and 150ml / ¼ pint water**

For this purpose the fruit must be used before it is quite ripe, and part of the stalk must be left on. Weigh the fruit, rejecting all that is in the least degree blemished, and put it into a lined saucepan with the sugar and water, which should have been previously boiled together to a syrup. Boil the fruit in this for about 10 minutes, remove it from the heat, and drain the greengages. The next day boil up the syrup, put in the fruit again, let it simmer for a few minutes, then drain the syrup away. Continue this process for 5 or 6 days, and the last time place the green-gages, when drained, on a fine sieve, and put them in an oven to dry. Keep them in a box, with paper between each layer, in a place free from damp.

GREENGAGE PULP
PRESERVED

Here again the process is as in preparing Apricot Pulp, page 97.

MIRABELLE PASTE

Mirabelle Paste is made in exactly the same way as Apricot Paste, page 97.

MIRABELLE PULP
PRESERVED

Proceed as in the preparation of Apricot Pulp, page 97.

PEACH PASTE

Peach Paste is prepared in the same manner as Apricot Paste, page 97. Success will depend greatly upon the sugar being heated to the right degree.

PEACH PULP
PRESERVED

The process is again as in preparing Apricot Pulp, page 97. Especial care in choosing the peaches is required.

PINEAPPLE
PRESERVED DRY

Pare and slice the pineapples finely, pile on a large dish, and sprinkle each layer liberally with caster sugar. Keep it in a hot closet, or put it daily for 7 or 8 days into a cool oven, turning it frequently. When quite dry, bake a few slices at a time in a moderately hot oven. When cold, pack them in airtight boxes with paper between each layer.

PLUM PASTE

Plum Paste is also made like Apricot Paste, the fruit being passed through a fine sieve, and the process finished as in preparing Apple Paste, page 97.

PLUMS
PRESERVED DRY

equal weight of plums and granulated sugar

Put half the sugar into a preserving-pan with the addition of 300ml / ½ pint of cold water to each 450g / 1lb of sugar, and boil to a thin syrup. Divide the plums, remove the stones, and put the fruit into the prepared syrup. Simmer gently until half cooked, then turn the whole into a bowl, cover, and let it remain thus until the following day. Strain the syrup into a preserving-pan, add the rest of the sugar, and boil to the 'Large Pearl' degree (105°C / 222°F). Allow it to cool slightly, put in the plums, simmer very gently until tender, then remove them very carefully to a deep dish and strain the syrup over them. Let the plums remain covered for 48 hours, drain well, spread them on large dishes in single layers, and when quite dry pack them in airtight tins with wax paper between the layers.

QUINCE PASTE

Quince Paste is prepared in exactly the same way as Apple Paste, page 97, substituting quinces for apples.

REDCURRANT PASTE

Prepare in the same manner as Blackcurrant Paste, page 98.

Syrups & Fruit Juices

Pour home-made syrups on desserts, mix them in cocktails, or add to iced water for refreshing drinks.

The aim in preparing syrups is to preserve the aroma or flavour of the fruits, flowers, or vegetables from which they are extracted.

The principal points or degrees to which syrups should be boiled are from the 'small thread' (102°C / 215°F) to the 'large pearl' (105°C / 222°F); for if insufficiently boiled, the syrup is apt to become cloudy and mouldy, and if over boiled it will become candied.

Great care should therefore be taken to boil the syrup to the precise point. If it should, accidentally, be boiled too much, and to too high a degree, add a little water and boil up again.

Note that all fruits containing pectin or vegetable jelly require to stand – after being mashed – for about 2 or 3 days, in order to ferment, and to prevent the syrup from becoming jelly when bottled.

ALMOND SYRUP

1 litre / 2 pints water
600g / 1¼lb ground almonds
200g / 7oz granulated sugar
45ml / 3 tbsp bitter almond extract

Boil the water in a large saucepan. Add the ground almonds and return to the boil. Remove from the heat and allow to cool completely. Squeeze the mixture through a jelly-bag or fine cloth. Place the resulting liquid in a large saucepan, add the other ingredients and boil until a thick syrup is achieved, stirring frequently. Allow to cool, then bottle, seal and store. This syrup is refreshing when mixed with iced water.

APRICOT SYRUP

*Apricot syrup makes an unusual dessert sauce to go
with pancakes, waffles and fruit fritters, as well as ice-cream.
Whip a little of the syrup with double cream and
use it to fill profiteroles or meringues.*

sound ripe apricots
800g / 1¾lb sugar for each 1 litre / 1¾ pints juice

Stone and halve the apricots then put them in a large heatproof bowl. Crack half the stones and stir the kernels into the fruit. Stand the bowl over a saucepan of water, as a bain marie, and simmer until the fruit is quite soft and the juice flows freely. Crush the fruit occasionally.

Strain the liquid through a scalded jelly bag or sieve lined with scalded muslin. Measure it and pour it into a preserving pan. Bring the juice to the boil, then lower the heat and simmer it for 20 minutes. Skim the syrup and leave to cool.

Add the brandy, then pour the syrup into thoroughly clean bottles, leaving 2cm / ¾ inch headspace. Tighten the caps, then loosen them by a quarter turn. Stand the bottles on a thick pad of newspaper in a deep saucepan and pour in cold water to come up to the top of the bottles. Wedge pieces of cardboard or crumpled foil between the bottles to keep them upright.

Heat the water to 77°C / 170°F and keep it at that temperature for 30 minutes. If the water is brought to 88°C / 190°F it must be maintained for 20 minutes.

Have ready a clean, dry wooden board. Transfer the bottles to it and tighten their caps immediately. Allow to cool, label and store in a cool, dark, dry cupboard.

BLACKBERRY SYRUP

**To each 450g / 1lb fruit allow 450g / 1lb preserving sugar
and 15ml / 1 tbsp cold water**

Place the fruit, sugar and water in a large jar with a close-fitting cover, stand the jar in a saucepan of boiling water, and cook gently for about 2 hours. Strain the juice, measure it, put it into a preserving-pan (preferably an enamelled one), and boil gently for about 20 minutes, skimming carefully meanwhile. To each 600ml / 1 pint of syrup add a small glass of brandy, let it become quite cold, then bottle for use.

CRANBERRY SYRUP

*Cranberry syrup has a rich, excellent fruity flavour with a bright colour.
Use it to pep up bought vanilla ice-cream or add it to chilled
custard to make an unusual fool. It also tastes good with pancakes,
waffles or steamed sponge puddings.*

**sound, ripe cranberries
800g / 1¾lb sugar for each 1 litre / 1¾ pints juice**

Place the fruit in a heatproof bowl and crush it with a wooden spoon. Stand the bowl over a saucepan of simmering water, as a bain marie. Cook gently for 2 hours. Check that the saucepan does not boil dry, adding more boiling water as necessary. Strain the liquid through a scalded jelly bag or sieve lined with scalded muslin. Measure carefully, pour into a saucepan and add sugar in the proportion given above. Bring to the boil, reduce the heat and cook for 15 minutes. Skim, then leave until cold.

Pour the syrup into thoroughly clean bottles, leaving 2cm / ¾ inch headspace. Tighten the caps, then loosen them by a quarter turn. Stand the bottles on a thick pad of newspaper in a deep saucepan and pour in cold water to come up to the top of the bottles. Wedge pieces of cardboard or crumpled foil between the bottles to keep them upright. Heat the water to 77°C / 170°F and keep it at that temperature for 30 minutes. If the water is brought to 88°C / 190°F it must be maintained for 20 minutes.

Have ready a clean, dry wooden board. Transfer the bottles to it and tighten their caps immediately. Allow to cool, label and store in a cool, dark, dry cupboard.

FREEZER TIP
Instead of bottling the syrup, pour it into suitable freezer containers and freeze when cold. Freezing is the easiest and safest storage method for syrups.

CURRANT SYRUP

Take some fresh, ripe currants, either white or red, pick them over, mash them in a basin and let them stand for 2 or 3 days. Strain the juice through a jelly-bag or cloth. Take 1.8kg / 4lb granulated sugar and let it dissolve in 1 litres / 2 pints of currant juice. Finish as for Raspberry Syrup, page 110.

Note: Some confectioners take the following fruit for making currant syrup: – 2.3g / 5lb redcurrants, 1.4kg / 3lb stoned cherries, and 450g / 1lb raspberries; mix, mash, and leave to ferment for 2 or 3 days.

GINGER SYRUP

Make a pint of plain syrup, and pour in a few drops of essence of ginger: add a little caramel colouring. Bottle when cold and seal.

LEMON SYRUP

Take 300ml / ½ pint of plain syrup, and 150ml / ¼ pint lemon juice. Let the juice settle, take off the thin skin which forms on the top, then strain through a jelly-bag. Now pour the lemon juice into the syrup, gently boil it to the 'Large Pearl' (105°C / 222°F), and remove the scum. Strain through a jelly-bag until clear. When cold, bottle and seal.

MAIDENHAIR
SYRUP

This clear syrup was very popular with Victorians. It has a distinctive, astringent flavour that is sometimes enhanced with orange-flower water. Capillaire refers to the fronds from the Maidenhair fern.

Take 50g / 2oz capillaire, cut up into little pieces, then infuse them in 900ml / 1½ pints boiling water, covering the pan over. After 2 hours' infusion strain it through a cloth, add 900g / 2lb caster sugar, and the white of an egg beaten up. Boil to the 'Large Pearl' (105°C / 222°F), then strain through muslin until clear. Bottle when cold.

MORELLO CHERRY
SYRUP

Take 1.8kg / 4lb sugar, dissolve it in 1 litre / 2 pints cherry juice, and proceed as in making Raspberry Syrup, page 110.

MULBERRY SYRUP

Take 2.3kg / 5lb sugar, dissolve it in 1.7 litres / 3 pints of mulberry juice, and finish as in making Raspberry Syrup, page 110.

ORANGE SYRUP

Proceed as for Lemon Syrup (page 108), substituting oranges for the lemons.

ORANGE-FLOWER SYRUP

Take 600ml / 1 pint plain syrup, boil it to the 'Small Crack' (143°C / 290°F), then pour in 300ml / ½ pint of orange-flower water. Boil for a minute or so, remove the scum, and then finish as for Lemon Syrup, page 108.

PLAIN SYRUP I

Take 450g / 1lb granulated sugar, dissolve it in 300ml / ½ pint of water, boil for a few minutes after the sugar is dissolved, withdraw from the heat, and remove the scum. Boil up again to the 'Large Pearl' (105°C / 222°F), remove, and strain through a jelly-bag until clear. When cold, bottle and tie down.

PLAIN SYRUP II

Take 450g / 1lb granulated sugar, dissolve it in 300ml / ½ pint of water, and boil for a few minutes after the sugar is dissolved. Withdraw from the heat and remove the scum. Put on the heat again, boil for another minute or so, and remove the scum. This produces a syrup equal to about the 'Small Thread' (102°C / 215°F).

RASPBERRY SYRUP

Take plenty of fresh raspberries, white or red, pick them over, mash in a basin and let them stand for 2–3 days. Strain the juice through a jelly-bag or cloth. Dissolve 1.8kg / 4lb sugar in 1 litre / 2 pints raspberry juice, put on the heat and boil for a few minutes. When the sugar is dissolved, take off the heat and remove the scum. Boil up again to the 'Large Pearl' (105°C / 222°F), remove from the heat and strain through a jelly-bag or cloth until clear. Bottle when cold and seal.

STRAWBERRY SYRUP

Proceed as for Raspberry Syrup (page 110), but substitute strawberries.

UNSWEETENED FRUIT JUICE FOR ICES

The juice of raspberries, strawberries, cherries and redcurrants may be preserved by boiling the juice in bottles for about 20 minutes in the same way as for unsweetened bottled fruits. The sugar can be added afterwards, or when the juice is wanted for use.

WELSH NECTAR

225g / ½lb raisins
450g / 1lb granulated sugar
2 small lemons
4.4 litres / 8 pints boiling water

Remove the rinds of the lemons as thinly as possible, and pour over them the boiling water. When cool, add the strained juice of the lemons, the raisins stoned and finely chopped, and the sugar. Cover; let the preparation remain for 5 days, stirring three or four times daily, then strain in to bottles. This beverage will keep good only a short time.

Pickles & Chutneys

*Sweet and tangy, these include useful pantry items
for serving with cheeses and cold meats.
Others make excellent accompaniments
for spicy food and other meals.*

PICKLES

Vinegar is the main preserving agent used in pickles, sometimes with sugar. Since vinegar is a strong preservative, preparing pickles is comparatively easy with none of the pitfalls involved in achieving a good jam or marmalade.

PREPARING PICKLES

Vegetables should be prepared according to type, then salted for several hours or overnight. Sprinkle salt over every layer of vegetables. This extracts excess liquid any bitter juices or very strong flavours. The salt should be rinsed off before pickling and the ingredients dried with absorbent kitchen paper. Brine solution may be used instead of salting vegetables.

Packing in Jars
Thoroughly clean and dry jars must be well filled without squashing the vegetables or other ingredients.

Vinegar
White or distilled vinegar, cider vinegar or white wine vinegar give pickles the best colour. Dark vinegars discolour the vegetables or fruit. The vinegar may be spiced, flavoured or sweetened as required.

Spiced vinegar may be used hot, immediately after straining, or cold. Opinions differ as to the best method but as a rule cold vinegar is always safest and should always be used for eggs and fruit whose texture may suffer from having boiling vinegar poured over them.

Pour the vinegar into the jars, shaking them gently to free any trapped air bubbles. Check the vinegar level about 24 hours after bottling the pickles, and add extra to cover the pickles if necessary.

Maturing
Leave the pickles to mature for 1–3 weeks before using. Pickled eggs (hard-boiled eggs which are simply shelled and packed in jars promptly after cooking) should be left for a week; onions and other vegetables for at least 2–3 weeks.

STORING PICKLES

Cover with airtight lids, making sure that the lids do not have any exposed metal which will react with the vinegar. Label and store in a cool, dark cupboard.

Pickled eggs and fruit keep for up to 3 months. Properly stored, most vegetables keep for 6–9 months. Red cabbage should be eaten within 6 months as it tends to soften and become limp with prolonged storage.

CHUTNEYS

PREPARING INGREDIENTS

As usual, the way in which ingredients are prepared depends on type. They should be chopped or even minced so that they eventually cook down to a thick pulp.

Peel, core and pips should be removed. Tomatoes are best peeled but this is not necessary if they are minced or very finely chopped.

Spices
Ground or whole spices may be added; usually a combination of both is used. Whole spices should be tied in a small piece of scalded muslin so that they may be removed after cooking and before potting. Cinnamon sticks are usually easy to spot in the cooked preserve, so these do not have to be tied in muslin.

Sugar
Brown sugar gives chutneys a good flavour and rich colour. For lighter fruit chutneys, granulated sugar may be preferred.

COOKING CHUTNEYS

Long, slow cooking is the secret of success. A stainless steel pan must be large enough to hold all the ingredients and allow room for them to simmer steadily and be stirred. Stir the mixture occasionally until the sugar dissolves, then bring the chutney to the boil and reduce the heat so that it simmers. Cover the pan and cook for the time recommended in the recipe or until the chutney has darkened and become thick and pulpy. Stir the mixture occasionally during cooking to prevent it sticking to the bottom of the pan.

If the chutney is too liquid at the end of the recommended cooking time, or when all the ingredients are well reduced, allow it to boil, without a lid on the pan, until some of the excess liquid has evaporated. Stir frequently to prevent the mixture burning on the base of the pan.

POTTING

Have thoroughly clean, hot jars ready on a large sheet of paper or folded tea-towel. You also need a tea-towel to hold or steady the jars, a jam funnel and a small jug. The jars must have airtight lids which will not react with the metal and you should have sufficient waxed paper discs to top each preserve.

Pot the chutney as soon as it is cooked, cover with waxed paper and put on airtight lids at once. Seal the lids in place with freezer tape. If for any reason the chutney is allowed to stand before potting, lids should not be put in the jars until the preserve is cold.

STORING

Store as for other preserves, in a cool, dark, dry cupboard. Most chutneys will keep well for up to a year.

SUCCESSFUL CHUTNEYS AND PICKLES

If a recipe involves boiling vinegar, an unchipped enamel pan is best since the acid in the vinegar may react badly with brass, copper or iron. For the same reason, use only wooden spoons for stirring. Pickles and chutneys should always be made from fresh, slightly underripe fruit and vegetables.

Vinegar should contain at least 5 per cent acetic acid and only the best quality should be used. Use fresh spices for a full flavour and remember, when tasting chutneys during the cooking process, that the mixture is always spicier when first made. The flavours will mellow over time. Pot pickles and chutneys in glass or stone jars and be sure that pickles are completely covered with vinegar before sealing the jar.

APPLES, PICKLED

1kg / 2¼lb thickly sliced apples
450g / 1lb brown sugar
350g / 12oz sultanas
15g / ½oz salt
15g / ½oz mustard seeds
15g / ½oz ground ginger
7.5g / ¼oz garlic, bruised
2.5ml / ½ tsp cayenne
600ml / 1 pint good vinegar

Simmer the vinegar, sugar and apples gently until reduced to a pulp, stir in the remaining ingredients, and, when well mixed, turn the whole into a basin. Cover, stir two or three times daily for 1 week, then bottle, and seal securely.

MRS BEETON'S TIP

White mustard seeds are not just a good flavouring; they are also a powerful preservative, which discourages the formation of moulds and bacteria in pickles and chutneys.

ARTICHOKES, PICKLED

Make a strong brine; when boiling put in the globe artichokes, boil gently for 10 or 15 minutes, and drain well. Remove and put aside the chokes, place the artichokes in jars, and cover them with boiling spiced vinegar. When cold, fill the jars with salad-oil, cover closely, and store.

BANANA CHUTNEY

30 small bananas
1 small onion, sliced
25–50g / 1–2oz chillies, chopped (see Mrs Beeton's Tip)
1.5 litres / 2½ pints white vinegar
225g / 8oz seedless raisins
50g / 2oz salt
50g / 2oz ground ginger
450g / 1lb soft light brown sugar

Slice the bananas into a large saucepan. Add the remaining ingredients, bring to the boil and cook over moderate heat for 2 hours, stirring occasionally. When the chutney reaches the desired consistency, pour into warm clean jars and cover with vinegar-proof lids. When cool, wipe the jars, label and store in a cool dry place.

MRS BEETON'S TIP

Leave the seeds in the chillies if you like a fiery chutney. For a milder result, remove them. Always take great care when working with chillies not to touch your lips or eyes; a strong reaction may occur on delicate skin. Wash your hands very carefully after chopping the chillies.

BEETROOT PICKLE I

6 medium-sized beetroots
1 litre / 2 pints malt vinegar
15g / ½oz whole black pepper
15g / ½oz allspice
1 small horseradish, grated
salt to taste

Wash the beetroots well, taking care not to break the skins, and bake them in a moderate oven for about 1½ hours. When cool enough to handle remove the skins, cut the beetroots into 1cm / ½ inch slices, and place them in jars. Meanwhile boil the vinegar, horseradish, pepper and spice together, let the mixture become quite cold, then pour in over the beetroot. Cover the jars closely and store in a cool, dry place.

BEETROOT PICKLE II

6 beetroots
1 litre / 2 pints vinegar
15g / ½oz whole pepper
15g / ½oz allspice

Wash the beetroots well, but take care to keep the skins intact, or they will lose some of their colouring. Put them into boiling water, cook gently for about 1½ hours, until they are three-quarters cooked, then drain them, and let them cool. Boil the spice, pepper and vinegar together, and put these aside until quite cold, meanwhile peel the beetroots, cut them into 1 cm / ½ inch slices, and place them in jars. Pour the cold prepared vinegar over them, cover closely, and store in a cool, dry place. The pickle will be ready for use in 1 week.

CABBAGE, PICKLED RED I

1 firm red cabbage
1 litre / 2 pints vinegar
15g / ½oz whole pepper
15g / ½oz allspice

Remove the outer leaves of the cabbage, quarter it, remove the centre stalk, and cut each section across into very fine strips. Pile the shredded cabbage on a large dish, sprinkle it liberally with salt, and let it remain thus until the following day. Meanwhile boil the vinegar, pepper and spice together, the latter being tied together in a piece of muslin, and allow the preparation to become quite cold. Turn the cabbage into an earthenware or enamelled colander, and when well drained put it into a large jar, and pour in the vinegar. It will be fit for use in 3 or 4 days; if kept for any length of time the cabbage loses the crispness and colour which are its chief recommendations.

CABBAGE, PICKLED RED II

1 firm red cabbage
1 litre / 2 pints malt vinegar
15g / ½oz black peppercorns
15g / ½oz allspice

Remove the outer leaves of the cabbage, quarter it, cut away the stalk from the centre, and shred the sections across as finely as possible. Put the prepared cabbage into a large jar, sprinkle each layer with salt, and press the whole lightly down. Boil the pepper and spice in the vinegar; when cold, pour it over the jars, and cover them closely. The pickle will be ready for use in 3 or 4 days; it may be kept for a considerable time, but after being pickled for 2 or 3 weeks it loses much of its crispness and colour.

CAULIFLOWER, PICKLED I

Select firm white cauliflowers and sufficient vinegar to cover them
To 1 litre / 2 pints vinegar allow 5ml / 1 tsp peppercorns,
5ml / 1 tsp allspice and 6 cloves

Break the cauliflowers into small florets, place them on a dish, sprinkle them liberally with salt, and let them remain thus for 6 hours. Meanwhile tie the seasoning ingredients in muslin, boil them in the vinegar for about half an hour, and allow it to become quite cold. Drain the cauliflowers well from the salt, place them in wide necked bottles or jars, and pour the prepared vinegar over them. Cover closely, store in a cool, dry place for about 1 month.

CAULIFLOWER, PICKLED II

Select firm white cauliflowers and sufficient vinegar to cover them
To each 1 litre / 2 pints vinegar allow 5ml / 1 tsp peppercorns
and 5ml / 1 tsp allspice

Tie the peppercorns and allspice in muslin, simmer these very gently in the vinegar for about 20 minutes, and put aside until quite cold. Have ready a saucepan of boiling, highly salted water, break the cauliflowers into small florets, throw them into the water, boil for 5 minutes, and drain well. When quite cold put them into wide necked bottles or jars, with a few peppercorns and a little allspice, cover with the prepared vinegar, and cover closely. They should be ready for use in 3 or 4 weeks.

CAULIFLOWER, PICKLED, WITH ONIONS

**Take an equal weight of cauliflower florets and silverskin
onions, and sufficient vinegar to cover
To each 1 litre / 2 pints vinegar allow
5ml / 1 tsp peppercorns, 5ml / 1 tsp allspice, 5 ml /
1 tsp black pepper, 1 blade mace, 25g / 1oz turmeric, 15ml /
1 tbsp curry powder, 15ml / 1 tbsp lemon juice,
and about 15ml / 1 tbsp lime juice**

Put as much water as will cover the cauliflower florets into a large saucepan; to
each 2 pints add 100g / 4oz of salt, boil for 10 minutes, and allow it to become
quite cold. Break the cauliflowers into small florets, cover them with the cold
brine, let them remain immersed for 3 days, then drain well. Peel the onions,
place them in jars or wide necked bottles in layers alternating with cauliflower
florets; sprinkle each layer with a little allspice, a few peppercorns, and 1 or
2 pieces of mace. Mix the black pepper, turmeric, curry powder, mustard and
salt, lemon juice and lime juice, to a smooth paste, add the vinegar gradually,
and pour the whole over the cauliflowers and onions. Cover closely, and store
in a cool, dry place. The pickle will be ready for use in 3 or 4 weeks.

CHERRIES, PICKLED I

**Select some sound, not overripe cherries
and sufficient vinegar to cover them
To each 600ml / 1 pint of vinegar allow
225g / ½lb sugar, cayenne to taste and
a few drops of red food colouring**

Pick the cherries carefully, rejecting those which are not quite sound, leave about
1 inch of their stalks, and put the fruit into jars. Boil the vinegar, add to it the
sugar and cayenne, skim well, let it boil for a few minutes, then turn it into a
bowl. When cold, add a few drops of carmine or cochineal, pour it over the cherries, cover the jars closely, and store in a cool, dry place until required for use.

CHERRIES, PICKLED II

**Select sound, not overripe cherries and sufficient vinegar to cover them
To each 2 pints vinegar allow 450g / 1lb sugar**

Leave 2.5cm / 1 inch of the stalks on the cherries, and pack them lightly in jars.
Boil the vinegar and sugar together, pour it whilst hot over the fruit, and when
cold tie paper over the jars. Let them stand in a cool place for 1 week, then drain
off the vinegar, boil and skim well, and again pour while hot over the fruit.
When cold cover closely, and keep in a cool, dry place.

COCKLES, PICKLED

The large cockles found on the north east coast are the best for this purpose.
Wash them in several waters to remove the grit; when quite free from it cover
the cockles with cold water, add a good handful each of salt and oatmeal, and
let them remain until the following day. To each 1 litre / 2 pints of cockles allow
a small 2.5ml / ½ tsp of allspice, and the same quantity of peppercorns. Tie these
spices in muslin and boil them for about 20 minutes in sufficient vinegar to
cover the cockles.

Put the cockles into a steamer, or, failing this, a large iron saucepan with 2 or
3 tablespoons of water to protect the bottom of the pan, cover them first with a
wet kitchen cloth, then the lid, and cook the cockles slowly until their shells
may be easily opened with the point of a knife (about 15 minutes). Put the cockles into the prepared cold vinegar, and the liquor contained in the shells into a
basin, and as soon as it is cold strain it into the vinegar. Cockles or oysters pickled in this way may be kept some days.

CORIANDER CHUTNEY

Unlike the other recipes in this section, this chutney must be served within a short time of being made. If stored in an airtight jar in the refrigerator, it will keep for up to 5 days. Serve it as an accompaniment to an Indian meal.

2 onions, finely chopped or grated
1 garlic clove, crushed
1 tomato, peeled and chopped
1 green chilli, chopped
1cm / ½ inch fresh root ginger, peeled and grated
15ml / 1 tbsp chopped fresh coriander leaves
45ml / 3 tbsp tomato ketchup
30ml / 2 tbsp vinegar
2.5ml / ½ tsp salt
1.25ml / ¼ tsp black peppercorns

Combine all the ingredients in a bowl. Mix well. Serve at once or store in the refrigerator as suggested above.

SERVES FOUR TO FIVE

VARIATION

For a smooth chutney, substitute 150ml / ¼ pint water for the vinegar and process in a blender or food processor.

MRS BEETON'S TIP

Fresh coriander, sometimes known as cilantro or Chinese parsley, is widely used in the East. Most countries use only the leaves, but the roots can be used in curry pastes, while the stalks are sometimes used for flavouring in Indian lentil and bean dishes.

CUCUMBERS, PICKLED I

Peel the cucumbers, cut them into 1cm / ½ inch slices, sprinkle them liberally with salt, and let them remain until the following day. Let the cucumber drain for at least 2 hours on a fine sieve, then place in wide-necked glass bottles. Boil sufficient vinegar to cover them, adding to each 600ml / 1 pint of vinegar 15g / ½oz of peppercorns, 15g / ½oz of allspice, and 2.5ml / ½ tsp salt, and pour it while hot over the cucumber, and cover closely.

CUCUMBERS, PICKLED II

Pare and slice the cucumbers thinly, sprinkle liberally with salt, and let them remain until the following day. Drain off the liquor, pack the slices closely in jars, sprinkling each layer thickly with salt, and cover closely. When wanted for use, wash well in cold water, drain well, and dress with pepper, vinegar and oil.

DAMSONS, PICKLED

3.2kg / 7lb sound, dry damson plums
1.8kg / 4lb preserving sugar
22.5g / ¾oz cinnamon stick
22.5g / ¾oz cloves
sufficient vinegar to cover

Remove the stalks but not the stems of the fruit, place them in layers in a large jar, sprinkle each layer with sugar, cinnamon and cloves. Cover the whole with vinegar, place the jar in a saucepan of boiling water, cook gently until the juice flows freely, then put the jar aside until the contents are quite cold. Then drain the syrup into a preserving-pan, bring to boiling-point, and pour it over the fruit. Repeat this process for 7 or 8 days, when the skins should be hard and the plums have a clear appearance. After the last boiling, transfer the plums to smaller jars. Boil the syrup, pour it over the plums, and when cold cover closely.

EGGS, PICKLED

16 eggs, hard boiled
1 litre / 2 pints vinegar
15g / ½oz black peppercorns
15g / ½oz allspice
15g / ½oz ginger

Remove the shells, and arrange the eggs compactly in wide-necked jars. Boil the peppercorns, spice and ginger in the vinegar until some of their flavour is extracted, and pour it whilst boiling hot over the eggs. When cold, cover closely, and store in a cool, dry place.

ENGLISH CHUTNEY

3 dozen sour apples
1.4kg / 3lb coarse brown sugar
225g / ½lb salt
900g / 2lb sultanas
100g / 4oz green ginger
100g / 4oz bird's-eye chillies
40g / 1½oz mustard seed
5 medium-sized Spanish onions
6 shallots
3.3 litres / 6 pints malt vinegar

Dissolve the salt and sugar in the vinegar, strain, and return it to the peserving-pan. Add the apples, onions and ginger all thinly sliced, the sultanas cleaned and picked, also the rest of the ingredients, and cook very gently until the apples and onions are quite tender. Pour into small jars or wide necked bottles; when cold, cover closely, and store in a cool, dry place.

EXCELLENT PICKLE
(For immediate use)

Place equal quantities of sliced onion, cucumber and sour apple in a dish in alternate layers, add salt and cayenne to taste. To 300ml / ½ pint of vinegar add 1 wineglassful each of sherry (optional) and soy and pour over. Let the pickle stand for a few hours before serving.

FRENCH BEANS, PICKLED

Cover the young French beans with strong brine, let them remain for 3 days, then drain. Place them in a saucepan with vine leaves under and over, cover with boiling salted water, cook gently for a few minutes, then drain and pack loosely in jars. Cover with boiling spiced vinegar, drain it off, and re-boil on two following days. The pickled beans should be kept closely covered in a cool, dry place.

FRENCH SOUR PICKLES

900g / 2lb pickling cucumbers
45ml / 3 tbsp pickling salt
2 litres / 3½ pints water
750ml / 1¼ pints white vinegar
4 small white onions, peeled
4 small garlic cloves, peeled
20ml / 4 tsp mustard seeds

Wash the cucumbers and slice off the very ends. Place the cucumbers in a large bowl, sprinkle them with salt and cover with water. Let this stand for 1 day. Drain well. Heat the vinegar in a medium saucepan until it boils.

Pack the cucumbers into 4 sterilized 600ml / 1 pint jars. Place 1 onion, 1 garlic clove, and 5ml / 1 tsp mustard seeds in each jar. Pour the boiling vinegar over cucumbers, filling the jars but leaving some headspace.

Boil the jars for 10 minutes. Remove the jars; cool them on wire racks for at least 12 hours, then store.

GHERKINS, PICKLED

Cover the gherkins with salt and water, and let them remain in the brine for 3 days. At the end of the time drain them well, dry them with a cloth, and pack them compactly in a jar of suitable size. Boil sufficient vinegar to cover them allowing to each 2 pints vinegar 7.5g / ¼oz of allspice, 7.5g / ¼oz of black peppercorns, 4 cloves and 2 blades of mace, for 10 minutes and pour the liquid over the gherkins.

Cover closely, let the jar stand in a warm place until the following day, then drain off the vinegar into a saucepan. Boil up, pour the vinegar at once over the gherkins, and let them remain covered until the following day. This process must be repeated daily until the gherkins are sufficiently green; they should then be put into wide-necked glass bottles, covered completely with vinegar, for which purpose it may be necessary to supplement that already used. They should be tightly sealed before being stored away.

GOOSEBERRY CHUTNEY

1 litre / 2 pints green gooseberries
275g / 10oz sultanas
1 onion
1 litre / 2 pints vinegar
40g / 1½oz ground ginger
40g / 1½oz mustard seed
75g / 3oz salt
225g / 8oz sugar
7.5g / ¼oz cayenne
15g / ½oz turmeric

Chop the gooseberries, sultanas and onion; put into the preserving-pan with the vinegar, ginger, mustard seed, salt, sugar, cayenne and turmeric. Boil gently for about 45 minutes, stirring occasionally. Bottle and seal.

HAMBURGER DILL CHIPS

1.8kg / 4lb pickling cucumbers
1 litre / 2 pints water
1 litre / 2 pints white vinegar
90ml / 6 tbsp salt
16 sprigs fresh dill
20ml / 4 tsp mustard seeds
16 peppercorns

Wash the cucumbers and slice off the very ends. Cut cucumbers into 5mm / ¼ inch slices. Combine water, vinegar, and salt in large saucepan and bring to the boil.

Pack the cucumbers in 8 sterilized 600ml / 1 pint jars. Add 2 dill sprigs, 2.5ml / ½ tsp mustard seeds, and 2 peppercorns to each jar. Pour boiling liquid over cucumbers, filling to within 5mm / ¼ inch from the top. Boil the jars for 15 minutes. Remove and cool for at least 12 hours.

INDIAN CHUTNEY

1 litre / 2 pints malt vinegar
450g / 1lb sour apples, peeled, cored and sliced
225g / ½lb onions, peeled and coarsely chopped
450g / 1lb soft brown sugar
225g / ½lb raisins, chopped
100g / 4oz salt
100g / 4oz ground ginger
50g / 2oz mustard powder
7.5g / ¼oz cayenne
4 small cloves garlic, finely chopped

Cook the apples, onions and garlic with the salt, sugar and vinegar until quite soft, and pass through a fine sieve. Add the raisins, ginger, cayenne and mustard, mix well, turn into a jar, and stand in a warm, but not hot, place overnight. Fill some dry, wide-necked small bottles or jars with chutney, and cover closely so as to exclude the air. This chutney may be kept for a year or two.

INDIAN CHUTNEY SAUCE

100g / 4oz sour apples, peeled, cored and sliced
100g / 4oz tomatoes, sliced
100g / 4oz salt
100g / 4oz brown sugar
100g / 4oz raisins
50g / 2oz cayenne
50g / 2oz ground ginger
25g / 1oz shallots
7.5g / ¼oz garlic
1.7 litres / 3 pints malt vinegar
600ml / 1 pint lemon juice

Mix all the ingredients together in a large jar. Cover the jar, keep in a moderately warm place for 1 month, and stir two or three times daily. At the end of the time strain off the liquor, let the residue drain well, but do not squeeze it. Pour into small bottles, seal tightly, and store in a cool, dry place.

INDIAN PICKLE

4.5 litres / 1 gallon vinegar
6 cloves garlic
12 shallots
2 sticks sliced horseradish
100g / 4oz fresh ginger, bruised
50g / 2oz whole black pepper
25g / 1oz allspice
12 cloves
7.5g / ¼oz cayenne
50g / 2oz mustard seed
100g / 4oz mustard
25g / 1oz turmeric
1 white cabbage
cauliflowers, radish pods, French beans, gherkins, small round
pickling onions, nasturtiums, peppers, chillies, etc.

Cut the cabbage, which must be hard and white, into slices, and the cauliflowers into florets; sprinkle with salt in a large dish, and leave for 2 days. Then dry the vegetables and put them into a very large jar with the garlic, shallots, horseradish, ginger, pepper, allspice and cloves. Boil sufficient vinegar to cover the ingredients, pour it over them, and, when cold, cover closely.

As the other ingredients ripen at different times, they may be added as they are ready; these will be radish pods, French beans, gherkins, small onions, nasturtiums, peppers, chillies, etc. As these are procured they must be first washed in a little cold vinegar, wiped, and then added to the other ingredients in the jar, taking care that they are covered by the vinegar. Should it be necessary to add more vinegar to the jar, do not omit to boil it first. When all ingredients are added, turn out into a large pan, thoroughly mix, put the vegetables into smaller jars, without the vinegar, then boil the vinegar again, adding as much more as will be required to fill the different jars, also cayenne, mustard seed, turmeric and mustard, which must be well mixed with a little cold vinegar, allowing the quantities named above to each gallon of vinegar. Pour the vinegar, boiling hot, over the pickle, and, when cold, cover and seal. If the pickle is wanted for immediate use, the vinegar should be boiled twice more, but the better plan is to make it during one season for use during the next. This pickle will keep for years, if care is taken that the vegetables are quite covered by the vinegar.

KIWI FRUIT CHUTNEY

12 kiwi fruit, peeled and chopped
2 lemons, peeled and roughly chopped
3 onions, grated
1 large banana
150g / 5oz sultanas or raisins
100g / 4oz preserved ginger
10ml / 2 tsp salt
5ml / 1 tsp ground ginger
225g / 8oz brown sugar
2.5ml / ½ tsp pepper
250–300 ml / 8 fl oz–½ pint vinegar

Combine the kiwi fruit, lemons and onions in a large saucepan. Slice the banana into the pan and stir in all the remaining ingredients, using just enough vinegar to cover. Bring to simmering point and simmer gently for 1½ hours, then mash with a potato masher.

Continue cooking until fairly thick, then pour into warm clean jars and cover with vinegar-proof lids. When cool, wipe the jars, label and store in a cool dry place.

MRS BEETON'S TIP

Although kiwi fruit is now associated with New Zealand, it originated in China and was for many years known as the Chinese gooseberry. An excellent source of vitamin C, the fruit is ready to eat when it is slightly soft to the touch. Firmer kiwi fruit – often cheaper than when fully ripe – can be used for this chutney.

LEMON PICKLE

12 lemons
450g / 1lb sea salt
100g / 4oz mustard seed (tied in muslin)
50g / 2oz garlic, peeled
15g / ½oz grated nutmeg
15g / ½oz ground mace
7.5g / ¼oz ground cloves
1. litres / 2 pints white wine vinegar

Remove the rinds of the lemons in thin slices, and put them aside to be afterwards dried and used for flavouring purposes. Leave all the pith on the lemons, cut them lengthwise and across, thus forming 4 quarters, sprinkle over them the salt, and place them singly on a large dish. Let the dish remain in a warm place until all the juice of the lemons has dried into the pith, then put them into a large jar. Add the rest of the ingredients, cover closely, and let it stand near the heat, but not on the stove, for 5 days. At the end of the time, cover, seal and place the jar in a cool, dry place. At the end of 3 months strain off the vinegar through a fine sieve, and press the fruit well to extract as much moisture as possible. Strain two or three times, and, when quite clear, bottle for use. Store in a cool, dry place.

LEMONS, PICKLED

Take 12 lemons and sufficient vinegar to cover
To each 2 pints vinegar allow 25g / 1oz mustard seed,
25g / 1oz whole ginger, 15g / ½oz peppercorns, about
15g / ½oz cloves, 7.5g / ¼oz mace and 7.5g / ¼oz chillies

Make a brine strong enough to float an egg, put in the lemons and allow them to soak for 6 days, stirring them two or three times daily. At the end of this time, put the lemons into a saucepan of boiling water and boil steadily for about 15 minutes. Drain well, allow them to become quite cold, and put them into jars. Boil the vinegar, spices, etc, together until sufficiently seasoned and flavoured, then pour the boiling hot mixture over the lemons and cover closely. They will be ready for use in 6 months and should be kept in a cool, dry place.

LIMES, PICKLED

(See Lemons, pickled, page 131)

MANGO CHUTNEY

5 slightly under-ripe mangoes, peeled, stoned and sliced
25g / 1oz salt
450ml / ¾ pint Spiced Vinegar (page 175)
5ml / 1 tsp cayenne pepper
25g / 1oz fresh root ginger, bruised
25g / 1oz whole black peppercorns
450g / 1lb Demerara sugar

Put the mango slices in a bowl. Sprinkle with the salt, cover and leave overnight. Next day, drain and rinse the fruit, drain it again and put in a large saucepan or preserving pan. Add the vinegar and cayenne, Tie the ginger and peppercorns in a muslin bag and add the bag to the pan. Bring the mixture to the boil, lower the heat and simmer for 15-20 minutes or until the mangoes are soft. Remove the spice bag and stir the sugar into the pan. Heat gently until the sugar has dissolved, then bring to the boil and boil rapidly until the chutney thickens, stirring all the time. Pour into warm clean jars and cover with vinegar-proof lids. When cool, wipe the jars. Label and store in a cool dry place.

MAKES ABOUT 1.5kg / 3¼lb

PRESSURE COOKER TIP

Reduce the quantity of vinegar to 375ml / 13 fl oz.
Put the mangoes in the cooker and add 250ml / 8 fl oz
of the vinegar with the cayenne and spice bag.
Bring it to the boil, cover and cook for 5 minutes at
15lb pressure. Reduce pressure quickly, remove the
spice bag and stir in the sugar and remaining vinegar.
Continue cooking in the open pan.

MANGO CHUTNEY, INDIAN

30 green mangoes
900g / 2lb sugar
225g / ½lb salt
900g / 2lb raisins
450g / 1lb green ginger
75g / 3oz dried chillies
100g / 4oz garlic
1.7 litres / 3 pints vinegar

Peel and slice the mangoes, chop them finely, also chop finely the raisins, green ginger and garlic. Pound the chillies in a mortar until smooth, then mix them with the rest of the prepared ingredients. Dissolve the sugar and salt in the vinegar, bring to the boil, then let it become quite cold and mix it with the mangoes, etc. Turn into wide-necked bottles or jars, cover closely, let them remain in the sun for 3 or 4 days, then store for use.

MANGO PICKLE, INDIAN

12 medium mangoes
300g / 11oz mustard powder
250g / 9oz red chili powder
200g / 7oz salt
50g / 2oz fenugreek seeds
1 litre / 2 pints sesame seed oil
garlic cloves to taste

Soak the mangoes in cold water for 15 minutes and dry them with a clean cloth. Cut them into 5-cm / 2-inch cubes. Discard the stones and dry the mango pieces with a clean tea-towel.

Mix the mustard powder, red chili powder, salt, garlic and fenugreek seeds together in a large bowl. Add the oil. Mix the mango pieces into this mixture a few at a time until they are incorporated. Cover closely and store for 3 days. Mix well on the fourth day, adding extra salt to taste, if needed.

MANGOES, PICKLED

Halve and stone the mangoes, stuff them with a mixture of sliced green ginger, mustard seed and bruised garlic, replace the halves, and fasten them securely with strong cotton. Cover the mangoes with boiling spiced vinegar. On the following day strain off the vinegar, re-boil, and repeat the process on the two following days, four times in all. When cold, turn the preparation into jars, cover closely, and store in a dry, cool place.

MELON PICKLE

Cut the melon into quarters, peel thinly, and remove the seedy parts. Shred the pieces rather coarsely, and put them in a jar. Sprinkle with salt, and let them stand for 5 or 6 hours. Next pour over some wine vinegar diluted with water. To every 450g / 1lb of melon, weighed when drained, allow 225g / 8oz of sugar, 600ml / 1 pint of vinegar, a cinnamon stick, a little grated horseradish and some mustard seeds. Cook these to the consistency of syrup, then add the drained melon. Pack in jars and cover them.

MELONS, PICKLED

Select some small melons, small French beans, grated horseradish, cloves, ground nutmeg, cinnamon, pepper, vinegar, and to each 1 litre / 2 pints add 5ml / 1 tsp each cloves, allspice and black peppercorns

Cut off one end, scoop out the inside of each melon, then replace and secure the end. Cover the melons with strong brine, let them remain undisturbed for 4 days, then drain and dry well. Sprinkle the inside of each melon liberally with cloves, cinnamon, nutmeg and pepper, and stuff them with well-seasoned French beans and horseradish. Replace and tie on the ends, and pack the melons in a large jar, keeping the cut ends uppermost. Boil the vinegar and spices together for about 10 minutes, and, when cold, pour the liquid over the melons. On three consecutive days re-boil the vinegar, and pour it boiling over the melons. When cold, cover closely, and store in a cool, dry place.

MILD CHILI SAUCE

12 ripe red peeled tomatoes
6 medium onions, chopped
6 green peppers, chopped
3 red sweet peppers, chopped
7.5cm / 3 inch stick cinnamon
5ml / 1 tsp whole cloves
5ml / 1 tsp whole allspice
15ml / 1 tbsp salt
600ml / 1 pint cider vinegar
250g / 9oz sugar

Peel the tomatoes by scoring their skins, dipping them in boiling water, then quickly plunging them in cold water. The skins should then come away easily.

Finely chop the tomatoes, onions and peppers. Tie the cinnamon, cloves, and allspice into a clean white cloth to make a spice bag. Add the spice bag to the chopped vegetables and simmer for 30 to 40 minutes. Remove the spice bag. Add salt, vinegar, and sugar to tomato mixture and boil rapidly for 5 minutes.

Pour chili sauce into clean, hot 600ml / 1 pint jars. Seal and boil the jars for 15 minutes. Remove jars, cool and store.

MIXED PICKLES I

Take an equal weight of small mild onions, sour apples and
cucumbers, and sufficient vinegar to cover
To each 600ml / pint of vinegar add 30ml / 2 tbsp sherry,
5ml / 1 tsp salt, 2.5ml / ½ tsp pepper, good pinch cayenne

Peel and slice the onions, apples and cucumbers thinly, put them into wide necked bottles, add the seasoning and sherry, cover with vinegar, and seal closely. This pickle may be used the following day, and should not be kept for any length of time.

MIXED PICKLES II

4.5 litres / 1 gallon vinegar
100g / 4oz ginger, bruised
100g / 4oz mustard
100g / 4oz salt
50g / 2oz mustard seeds
40g / 1¼oz turmeric
25g / 1oz ground black pepper
7.5g / ¼oz cayenne
cauliflowers, onions, celery, gherkins,
French beans, nasturtiums, peppers

Have a large jar, with a tight-fitting lid, in which put as much vinegar as required, reserving a little to mix the various powders to a smooth paste. Put into a basin the mustard, turmeric, pepper and cayenne; mix them with vinegar, and stir well until no lumps remain; add all the ingredients to the vinegar, and mix well. Keep this liquor in a warm place, and thoroughly stir it every morning for 1 month with a wooden spoon, when it will be ready for the different vegetables to be added to it.

As these come in season, and after merely wiping them with a cloth, to free them from moisture, put them into the pickle. The cauliflowers must be divided into small bunches. Put all these into the pickle raw, and at the end of the season, when as many of the vegetables as could be procured have been added, store the pickle away in jars. The pickle should always be kept for at least 3 months in a cool, dry place before being used.

MIXED PICKLES III

450g / 1lb onions
450g / 1lb apples
100g / 4oz chillies
900ml / 1½ pints white wine vinegar
15ml / 1 tbsp salt

Chop the onions and apples coarsely, and the chillies finely. Boil the vinegar, add the salt, and when dissolved pour over the prepared ingredients. Turn into small jars, and, when cold, cover closely.

MUSHROOMS, BOTTLED

Procure about 900g / 2lb of small button mushrooms and wipe them with a clean, dry cloth. Peel carefully, and trim off the stalks. Put the mushrooms into a basin and sprinkle with salt. Pour some well-diluted wine vinegar over the mushrooms and bring slowly to the boil. Shake them well, pour off the liquid and drain them. Then boil the mushrooms again, using a fresh lot of diluted vinegar. Remove the pan from the heat as soon as boiling and bottle the mushrooms as soon as they are cool, with enough vinegar to well cover. Seal the bottles, wrap them round with newspaper and steam or boil from 2 to 3 hours according to size.

Large mushrooms may be treated in exactly the same manner, but the red portion of the stalks should be removed. Mushrooms which are black round the stalks are unsuitable for preserving.

MUSHROOMS, PICKLED

1 litre / 2 pints button mushrooms
salt
1 litre / 2 pints vinegar
25g / 1oz whole ginger, bruised
15g / ½oz white peppercorns
3 blades mace

Wash, dry, and peel mushrooms and cut off the tops of the stalks. Place them in a preserving-pan, sprinkle with salt to taste, shake them over the heat until the liquor flows, and keep them on the stove uncovered until the greater part of the moisture has evaporated. Then add vinegar, ginger, white peppercorns and mace, bring to the boil, and simmer gently for about 10 minutes. Turn into jars, cover closely, and store in a cool, dry place.

MUSHROOMS, PRESERVED

To each 1 litre / 2 pints mushrooms allow 75g / 3oz butter,
pepper and salt to taste, juice of 1 lemon and clarified butter

Peel the mushrooms, put them into cold water, with a little lemon juice; let them remain for about 10 minutes, then dry them very carefully in a cloth. Put the butter into a preserving-pan capable of holding the mushrooms; when it is melted, add the mushrooms, lemon juice, and a seasoning of pepper and salt. Draw them down over a gentle heat, and let them remain until their liquor is boiled away, and they have become quite dry, but they must not stick to the bottom of the preserving-pan. When done, put the mushrooms into pots, and over the top pour clarified butter. If not wanted for immediate use, they will keep good a few days without being covered over. To re-warm them, put the mushrooms into a preserving-pan, strain the butter from them, and they will be ready for use.

MUSHROOMS
TO KEEP TEMPORARILY

Peel, wash, and thoroughly dry 1 litre / 2 pints mushrooms. Heat 50g / 2oz of butter in a large preserving-pan, put in the mushrooms, season lightly with salt and pepper, and add 15ml / 1 tbsp lemon juice. Leave the pan uncovered, and cook the mushrooms very slowly, until they become quite dry. They will keep good for several days, and when required for use should be reheated and drained free from butter. They may also be kept for some time if closely packed in a shallow pie-dish, and covered with clarified butter.

NASTURTIUM SEEDS, PICKLED

Take some nasturtium seeds and sufficient vinegar to cover
To each 600ml / 1 pint of vinegar add 15g / ½oz salt and 6 peppercorns

Boil the vinegar, salt and peppercorns together, and, when cold, strain it into a wide necked bottle. Gather the seeds on a dry day, put them into the vinegar, and seal closely. These pickled seeds form an excellent substitute for capers. They are ready for use in about 3 months, but may be kept for a much longer time with perfect safety.

MRS BEETON'S TIP

It is important to use small jars so that the contents can be used up quickly when opened.

ONION JAM

100g / 4oz butter
1kg / 2¼lb onions, in 1cm / ¼ inch slices
5ml / 1 tsp salt
2.5 ml / ½ tsp freshly ground black pepper
100g / 4oz sugar
30ml / 2 tbsp sherry
30ml / 2 tbsp red wine vinegar
250ml / ¼ pint red wine
50ml / 2 fl oz honey
100g / 4oz chopped dried prunes

Fry the onion slices in the butter and salt and pepper, over a very low heat, for thirty minutes.

Mix in the sugar, sherry, red wine vinegar, red wine, honey and prunes. Cook over a very low heat, stirring frequently, for approximately 2 hours, until dark and thickened. This relish keeps in the refrigerator for up to two months.

ONIONS, PICKLED I

Take some pickling onions and sufficient vinegar to cover
To each 1 litre / 2 pints vinegar add 10ml / 2 tsp each
allspice and whole black pepper

Have the onions gather when quite dry and ripe, and, with the fingers, take off the thin outer skin; then with a silver knife (steel should not be used, as it spoils the colour of the onions) remove one more skin, when the onions will look quite clear. Have ready some very dry bottles or jars, and as fast as the onions are peeled put them in. Pour over sufficient cold vinegar to cover them, with pepper and allspice in the above proportions, taking care that each jar has its share of the latter ingredients. Seal and put them in a dry place, and in a fortnight they will be ready for use.

MRS BEETON'S TIP

Allspice is a berry grown in the Caribbean. Its name derives from the flavour, which resembles a blend of cinnamon, nutmeg and cloves. It is added whole to pickles, chutneys, stews and marinades, while the ground form is used in all foods, especially cakes and puddings.

ONIONS, PICKLED II

Take some silverskin onions and sufficient white wine vinegar to cover

Remove the skins, throw the onions a few at a time into a saucepan of boiling water, taking care to have no more than will form a single layer floating on the surface of the water. As soon as the onions look clear on the outside take them up as quickly as possible with a slice, fold them in a clean dry cloth, so as to keep in the steam, and allow them to remain closely covered until the whole have been scalded. Let the onions be until quite cold, then put them into bottles or jars, and pour over them the vinegar, which should previously have been boiled and allowed to cool slightly. When cold, cover closely, and store in a cool, dry place.

ONIONS, PICKLED (SPANISH)

Peel some medium sized onions, slice them thinly, place them in a large jar, and sprinkle each layer liberally with salt, and lightly with cayenne pepper. Cover the whole with vinegar, exclude the air and store in a cool, dry place. The pickle will be ready for use in 10 or 14 days.

OYSTERS, PICKLED

Follow directions for Cockles, Pickled, page 121.

PEACH PICKLE I

1.8kg / 4lb ripe peaches
2.2 litres / 4 pints pale brown vinegar
10ml / 2 tsp whole mixed peppercorns
2 red chillies, chopped
10ml / 2 tsp coriander seeds
10ml / 2 tsp mustard seeds
5-cm / 2-inch piece root ginger
15g / ½oz curry powder
225g / 8oz brown sugar
50–75g / 2–3oz salt
2–3 onions, minced

Halve and stone peaches. Boil vinegar with peppercorns, chillies, coriander seeds, mustard seeds, ginger, curry powder, brown sugar and salt. Fry onions in oil to a light brown only, then add to the mixture. Add in the peaches as soon as the syrup boils up, and cook until quite done. Store in the usual manner.

PEACH PICKLE II

900g / 2lb dried peaches
225g / ½lb brown sugar
225g / ½lb salt
50g / 2oz curry powder
6 large onions, sliced
6 chillies, shredded
6 large pieces ginger
15ml / 1 tbsp pepper
15ml / 1 tbsp mustard seeds
15ml / 1 tbsp coriander seeds
3.3 litres / 6 pints vinegar

Pour the vinegar over the peaches and let them soak for at least 12 hours. Fry the sliced onions in salad oil until well browned, and drain well. Pound or crush the spices. Boil all together until the peaches are quite soft but unbroken, then turn into jars, cover closely, and store for future use.

PEARS, SWEET, PICKLED

To each 450g / 1lb firm pears allow 225g / ½lb brown sugar,
150ml / ¼ pint malt vinegar, cloves, cinnamon and allspice

Peel the pears and tie the spices in muslin. Place the vinegar, sugar and spices in muslin. Place the vinegar, sugar and spices in a preserving-pan; when boiling add the pears, and cook them gently until tender. Remove the pears to a bowl or large basin, boil the syrup for about 10 minutes longer, then pour it over the fruit. On the following day boil up the syrup, and repeat the process the two following days. On the third day place the pears in jars or wide necked bottles, and remove the spices before adding the vinegar to the fruit. Store in a dry, cool place.

PEPERONATA

Served at room temperature, this Italian relish is delicious with pasta, on pizzas, or as an accompaniment to meat or poultry.

60ml / 2 fl oz oil
4 medium onions, finely sliced
5 sweet peppers (a combination of colours works well),
seeded and cut into fine strips
125ml / 4 fl oz water
125ml / 4 fl oz chopped parsley
4 garlic cloves, chopped
15ml / 1 tbsp sugar
30ml / 2 tbsp drained capers
30ml / 2 tbsp white wine vinegar
salt and pepper to taste

Fry the onion over a medium heat in a large saucepan, until tender and transparent. Add the pepper strips and water and simmer for 10 minutes, stirring occasionally, until the peppers are soft.

Mix in the parsley and garlic, sugar, drained capers and vinegar, salt and pepper, and bring to the boil. Lower the heat and simmer for 10 minutes.

Allow the mixture to cool completely. Refrigerated peperonata will keep for five days, or in sterilized jars for up to two months.

PEPPERS, PICKLED I

If the peppers can be obtained from the garden, they should be gathered when they are just at the point of turning red. To each 2 pints vinegar allow 5ml / 1 tsp of salt, and 1.25 ml / ¼ tsp of mace and nutmeg mixed in equal proportions. Slit the peppers at the side, take out the seeds, put the peppers into a jar, and sprinkle over them the salt, mace and nutmeg. Boil the vinegar, pour it at once upon the pods, and, when cold, cover closely. They will be ready for use in 4 or 5 weeks.

PEPPERS, PICKLED II

**Select young green peppers and to each 2 pints vinegar allow
5ml / 1 tsp salt and 1.25ml / ¼ tsp ground mace**

Remove the stalks, scald the peppers, and let them remain under pressure for 24 hours, to extract some of their bitter water. Pack the peppers closely in a jar, pour over them boiling vinegar seasoned with salt and mace, and, when quite cold, cover closely. They will be ready for use in 5 or 6 weeks.

PICCALILLI

**Select some cauliflowers, onions, gherkins,
French beans and peppers**

Divide the vegetables into convenient pieces, throw them into boiling brine sufficiently strong to float an egg, and cook for 3 minutes. Drain well, spread them on large dishes, and let them remain in the sun until perfectly dry. Prepare sufficient spiced vinegar and add 15g / ½oz each of turmeric and curry powder to each 1 litre / 2 pints vinegar. Also allow to each 1 litre / 2 pints vinegar 25g / 1oz of mustard, which must be mixed smoothly with a little cold vinegar, and afterwards stirred into the boiling vinegar, but not allowed to boil. Place the prepared vegetables in jars, cover them completely with vinegar, and when quite cold cover closely.

PLUM PICKLE

The plums for this pickle must be ripe, but absolutely sound. Wipe them, prick them freely with a needle, and pack loosely into jars of about a 1-litre / 2-pint capacity. Three fourths fill them only with the fruit. Have ready the pickle made by boiling 1.7 litres / 3 level pints of granulated sugar with 1 litre / 2 pints vinegar to a syrup, adding to this quantity 18 cloves, 3 inches of stick cinnamon, broken up, 12 black peppercorns, and 5ml / 1 tsp allspice berries. These are to be bruised and left in the pickle. The jars must be filled, covered and stored in a cool, dry place.

PLUMS, SPICED

Prick the plums well with a fork, place them in a large jar with cinnamon, cloves and orange-rind between each layer. Cover with vinegar, and, on the following day, strain off and boil for about 10 minutes. Let it cool, pour it over the fruit and at the end of 24 hours again strain and measure it. To each 600ml / 1 pint add 75g / 3oz of sugar, boil the two together for 10 minutes, pour it over the plums, and, when cold, cover closely, and store in a dry, cool place.

RADISH-PODS, PICKLED

Cover some young radish-pods with strong brine, let them remain for 12 hours, then drain the brine into a saucepan, and boil up. Pour the boiling brine over the pods, cover closely with a close-fitting lid or plate, let them remain undisturbed for 48 hours, then repeat the boiling process. Repeat again and again until the pods are perfectly green, then drain until they are quite dry, and pack them loosely in jars. Add 30–45ml / 2–3 tbsp grated horseradish to sufficient prepared and spiced vinegar, pour it boiling over the pods, and cover closely. On the following day strain, boil and replace the vinegar, and, when quite cold, cover securely and store in a dry, cool place.

SALSA

2.27kg / 5lb ripe red tomatoes
900g / 2lb hot red or green chili peppers
450g / 1lb onions
250ml / 8 fl oz vinegar
15ml / 1 tbsp salt
2.5ml / 1 tbsp pepper

Purée and sieve the tomatoes. Finely chop the chili peppers and onions and mix all the ingredients into a large saucepan. Bring to the boil then leave to simmer for 10 minutes. Ladle the hot sauce into sterilized jars, leaving some head space, and seal. Boil the jars for 15 minutes, cool completely, then label and store.

SHALLOT OR GARLIC PICKLE

2.2 litres / 4 pints white wine vinegar
225g / ½lb shallots or garlic
50g / 2oz whole ginger
50g / 2oz chillies
100g / 4oz mustard seed
50g / 2oz turmeric

Cover the ginger with strong brine made by boiling together 600ml / 1 pint of water and 175g / 6oz of salt, let it remain for 5 days, then slice it thinly, and dry it in the sun. Peel the shallots or garlic, sprinkle liberally with salt, and let them remain thus for 3 days. Place the ginger, shallots, chillies, mustard-seed and turmeric in a wide-necked bottle, pour in the vinegar, cover closely, and store in a dry, cool place.

SWEET PICKLE

3.2 kg / 7lb peaches, pears or plums
1.8kg / 4lb preserving sugar
600ml / 1 pint vinegar
1 blade mace
1cm / ½ inch cinnamon
3 cloves

Remove skins, stones or cores of the fruit, and place the fruit in a preserving-pan with alternate layers of sugar. Bring very slowly to boiling point, then add the vinegar and spices, and boil for a few minutes. Take out the fruit with a skimmer, draining it well from the syrup, and place it on dishes to cool. Boil the syrup gently until thick, removing any scum as it rises, and pour it boiling over the fruit, which should be previously packed closely in glass jars. Seal tightly, and store in a cool, dry place.

SWEETCORN RELISH

2 green peppers, seeded and diced
2 large carrots, diced
2 large onions, chopped
6 celery sticks, diced
salt
2 garlic cloves, crushed
30ml / 2tbsp mustard powder
5ml / 1 tsp turmeric
15ml / 1 tbsp cornflour
600ml / 1 pint white vinegar
900g / 2lb fresh or thawed frozen sweetcorn kernels
100g / 4oz sugar

Place the peppers, carrots, chopped onion and celery in a bowl, sprinkling each layer with a little salt. Sprinkle more salt on top of the vegetables, cover the bowl and leave them to stand overnight.

Next day, drain, rinse, drain again and dry the vegetables, then place them in a large saucepan with the garlic. In a cup, blend the mustard, turmeric and cornflour to a paste with a little of the vinegar. Pour the rest of the vinegar into the pan and bring the vegetable mixture to the boil.

Reduce the heat and cover the pan, then simmer the mixture for 5 minutes. Add the sweetcorn and cook, covered, for a further 5 minutes. Stir in the sugar and cook gently, stirring, until it has dissolved.

Spoon a little of the hot liquid into the mustard mixture, then stir the thin paste into the relish. Add 5ml / 1 tsp salt and stir well. Bring to the boil, stirring all the time, then lower the heat and simmer steadily for 5 minutes without a lid on the pan. Pot and cover at once, then label and store for at least a week. The relish will keep for 6–9 months.

SWEETCORN, PICKLED

Boil the corn in salt and water, drain well and cover with spiced vinegar. When cold, seal securely, and store in a dry, cool place.

TOMATOES, PICKLED

Prepare some spiced vinegar, and to each 1 litre / 2 pints add 10ml / 2 tsp of moist sugar. Pack some small firm tomatoes loosely in a large jar, cover them with boiling vinegar, and put on a close fitting lid or plate to keep in the steam. Cover to exclude the air completely. This pickle will only keep for a short time.

TOMATO CHOW CHOW

6 large tomatoes
1 Spanish onion
1 green pepper
30ml / 2 tbsp brown sugar
15ml / 1 tbsp salt
300ml / ½ pint vinegar.

Peel and chop the onion coarsely. Blanch the tomatoes, remove the skins, and slice them finely. Place the onion and tomatoes in a casserole dish, add the pepper finely chopped, the sugar, salt and vinegar, and cook in a slow oven until the onion is quite tender. When cold turn into small jars or wide-necked bottles, cover closely, and store in a cool, dry place.

TOMATO CHUTNEY

2.7kg / 6lb ripe tomatoes
1.4kg / 3lb sour cooking apples, peeled, cored and finely chopped
100g / 4oz salt
225g / 8oz brown sugar
1.7 litres / 3 pints vinegar
6 cloves garlic, chopped finely
50g / 2oz ground ginger
25g / 1oz mustard seed

Scald the tomatoes, remove skins, cut them into slices, and put them into a cooking pot with the vinegar, salt and apples. When the fruit is soft, rub through a sieve, add the sugar, ginger, garlic and mustard seed, and boil the whole gently for 30–45 minutes. Pour the contents of the cooking pot into a dish, cover it, and let it stand in a warm place for about 3 days. Bottle the chutney and seal tightly to exclude the air. Sultanas or preserved ginger are sometimes added to the above ingredients.

TOMATO CONSERVE

1.4kg / 3lb ripe tomatoes
300ml / ½ pint vinegar
10ml / 2 tsp caster sugar
5ml / 1 tsp ground ginger
3.5g / ⅛oz garlic
2.5ml / ½ tsp allspice
10ml / 2 tsp salt

Bake the tomatoes in the oven until quite tender, then skin and place them in a jar or casserole dish with the above mentioned flavouring ingredients. Mix all together thoroughly and keep in a cool place for a few days. Then rub the tomato pulp through a fine sieve and boil up with a little more vinegar than sugar. Bottle when cool, seal the bottles and store them away in a cool, dry place until required for use. Peppers, shallots and lemon juice may be added if liked, but the conserve then becomes more of a condiment than a simple tomato conserve with its own natural flavour.

TOMATO PRESERVE

3.2kg / 7lb firm, ripe tomatoes
1.6kg / 3½lb sugar
25g / 1oz each cloves, allspice and cinnamon
600ml / 1 pint vinegar

Scald, drain and peel the tomatoes. Tie the spices in muslin, boil them for about 5 minutes with the sugar in the vinegar, then add the tomatoes, and simmer very gently for about half an hour. Keep closely covered in a dry, cool place.

VEGETABLES
PRESERVED

Nearly every kind of vegetable may be preserved by steaming in salt water and then filling into jars. After sealing the bottles stand them upside down to see if they leak.

VEGETABLE MARROWS, PICKLED

Select young vegetable marrows and sufficient vinegar to cover
To each 1 litre / 2 pints vinegar add 100g / 4oz sugar,
40g / 1¼oz ginger, broken into small pieces, 35g / 1¼oz mustard
powder, 15g / ½oz turmeric, 6 chillies and 1 clove garlic,
finely chopped

Boil the vinegar with the seasoning and flavouring ingredients until some of their strength and flavour is extracted. Meanwhile pare the marrows, cut them into 5-cm / 2-inch pieces, and remove the seeds. Add them to the boiling vinegar, cook gently for about 10 minutes, and turn into a large basin. When quite cold lift the pieces of marrow carefully into wide-necked bottles or unglazed jars, pour in the vinegar, and cover closely. The pickle will be ready in 2 or 3 weeks, and should be kept in a cool, dry place until required.

WALNUTS, PICKLED I

Select some green walnuts and sufficient vinegar to cover
To each 1 litre / 2 pints vinegar allow 25g / 1oz peppercorns,
25g / 1oz allspice and 5ml / 1 tsp salt

Prick the walnuts well with a steel fork or large needle, put them into a pan, and cover them with strong cold brine previously made by boiling the necessary quantity of water with the addition of 100g / 4oz of salt to each 1 litre / 2 pints water. Stir the walnuts two or three times daily for 6 days, then drain them and cover with fresh brine. Let them remain 3 days, then again drain them, spread them on large dishes, and place them in the sun until quite cold pour the mixture over the walnuts. If closely covered and stored in a dry, cool place, they may be kept for months.

WALNUTS, PICKLED II

Select some green walnuts and sufficient vinegar to cover
To 1.7 litres / 3 pints vinegar allow 25g / 1oz salt and 15g / ½oz
each allspice, peppercorns, cloves and whole ginger

Wipe the walnuts with a dry cloth, put them into wide-necked bottles, or unglazed jars, and cover them with cold vinegar. Cover closely, let them stand in a cool, dry place for 4 months, then drain off the vinegar. Boil as much fresh vinegar as will cover them, with the seasonings as stated above, and pour it, while boiling hot, over the walnuts. Cover closely, and store for 3 weeks in a cool, dry place, the walnuts will then be ready for use.

MRS BEETON'S TIP

Always wear gloves when
handling walnuts, to
avoid staining.

Condiments
& Sauces

*Delicious ways to pep up meat, fish,
vegetables, salads and dairy.*

ANCHOVY ESSENCE

450g / 1lb anchovies
600ml / 1 pint cold water
150ml / ¼ pint vinegar
2.5ml / ½ tsp ground mace
2.5ml / ½ tsp cayenne

Pound the anchovies in a mortar until smooth, and pass them through a fine sieve. Put the parts that will not pass through the sieve into a preserving-pan, add any liquor there may be in the bottles from which the anchovies were taken, the mace, cayenne, and water, simmer gently for about ½ an hour, then strain, and mix it with the anchovy purée. Return the mixture to the pan, bring to boiling point, add the vinegar, simmer very gently for about 10 minutes longer, and when quite cold pour into small bottles. Seal securely and store for use in a cool, dry place.

ANCHOVY KETCHUP

1 litre / 2 pints good ale
100g / ¼lb anchovies
3 shallots, finely chopped
45ml / 3 tbsp mushroom ketchup
2.5ml / ½ tsp caster sugar
2.5ml / ½ tsp ground ginger
1.25ml / ¼ tsp ground mace
2 cloves

Put all the ingredients into a preserving-pan, simmer very gently for about 1 hour, and strain. When quite cold, pour the ketchup into small bottles, seal them tightly, and store in a cool, dry place.

BENTON SAUCE

(for hot or cold roast beef)

Mix 60ml / 4 tbsp vinegar, 15ml / 1 tbsp scraped horseradish, 5ml / 1 tsp mustard and 5ml / 1 tsp caster sugar well together, and serve.

BOAR'S HEAD SAUCE

(For game or cold meat)

300ml / ½ pint dissolved redcurrant jelly
small glass port
4 oranges
25g / 1oz sugar
1 shallot, finely chopped
2.5ml / ½ tsp mixed mustard
pepper

Shred the rind of 2 oranges into very fine strips, and rub the lumps of sugar over the rinds of the remaining two. Put the rind and sugar into the liquid jelly, add the wine, shallot, mustard, and a liberal seasoning of pepper, and use as required, or the sauce may be sealed into bottles and stored for use.

BROWN SAUCE

1.5kg / 3¼lb tomatoes, chopped
100g / 4oz onions, finely chopped
225g / 8oz soft light brown sugar
225g / 8oz raisins
75–100g / 3–4oz salt
25g / 1oz ground ginger
1.25ml / ¼ tsp cayenne pepper
1 litre / 1¾ pints malt vinegar

Combine all the ingredients in a large saucepan or preserving pan. Heat gently, stirring until all the sugar is dissolved, then raise the heat slightly and cook until the tomatoes and onions are soft.

Rub the mixture through a nylon or stainless steel sieve, then return it to the clean pan. Place over gentle heat and simmer until the sauce reaches the desired consistency.

Fill hot bottles, leaving a 2cm / ¾ inch headspace. The sauce will thicken on cooling, so do not reduce it too much. Seal the bottles immediately. Alternatively, allow the sauce to cool slightly, then fill the bottles (leaving a headspace) and sterilize at 88°C / 190°F for 30 minutes. Seal immediately. Label when cold.

CAMBRIDGE SAUCE

(For roast duck, cold meat, etc)

30ml / 2 tbsp olive oil
45ml / 3 tbsp tarragon vinegar
4 hard boiled egg yolks
4 anchovy fillets
15ml / 1 tbsp capers
10ml / 2 tsp French mustard
5ml / 1 tsp English mustard
5ml / 1 tsp finely chopped parsley
sprig tarragon
sprig chervil
pinch cayenne

Pound all the ingredients except the parsley well together, then pass through a fine sieve. If too stiff, add a little oil and vinegar gradually until the consistency resembles that of mayonnaise. Stir in the parsley and keep on ice until required.

CAMP VINEGAR

1 head garlic
15g / ½oz cayenne
10ml / 2 tsp soy sauce
30ml / 2 tbsp walnut ketchup
600ml / 1 pint vinegar
few drops red food colouring

Slice the garlic, and put it, with all the above ingredients, into a clean bottle. Let it stand to infuse for 1 month, then strain it off quite clear, and it will be fit for use. Keep it in small bottles, well sealed to exclude the air.

CARRACK SAUCE

(For cold meat)

Mix 1 litre / 2 pints vinegar, 50ml / 2 fl oz mushroom ketchup, 50ml / 2 fl oz soy, 80ml / 3 fl oz coarsely-chopped pickled walnuts, 30 ml / 1 fl oz coarsely-chopped mango pickle, 15g / ½oz of garlic bruised, and 15 anchovies finely chopped well together in a bottle, let it remain in a warm place, and shake it daily for a month, when it will be ready.

CAYENNE VINEGAR

Mix 2.2 litres / 4 pints vinegar and 40g / 1½oz of cayenne pepper together in a bottle, let it stand for 1 month, shaking the preparation daily. When ready, strain into clean, dry bottles, seal them and store for use.

CELERY VINEGAR

**225g / ½lb celery, finely shredded,
or 15g / ½oz celery seeds
600ml / 1 pint pickling vinegar
5ml / 1 tsp salt**

Boil the vinegar, dissolve the salt in it, and pour the mixture over the celery or celery seed. When cold, cover and let it remain undisturbed for 3 weeks, strain into small bottles, and seal securely.

CHEROKEE

Put 1 litre / 2 pints best malt vinegar, 300ml / ½ pint of walnut ketchup, 60ml / 4 tbsp soy, 25g / 1oz of cayenne, and 3 minced cloves of garlic into a large bottle, seal tightly, and let them remain undisturbed for 1 month. At the end of this time, strain the liquid into small bottles, seal securely and store.

CHILLI VINEGAR

50 fresh chillies
600ml / 1 pint pickling vinegar

Cut the chillies in halves. Boil the vinegar, let it become quite cold, then pour it over the chillies. Seal closely, and store.

CRANBERRY KETCHUP

1kg / 2¾lb cranberries
2 onions, finely chopped
5ml / 1 tsp mustard seeds
1 cinnamon stick
1cm / ½ inch fresh root ginger, bruised
2.5ml / ½ tsp peppercorns
2 bay leaves
15ml / 1 tbsp salt
250ml / 8 fl oz white vinegar
450g / 1lb white sugar

Put the cranberries and onions in a large saucepan or preserving pan. Add 250ml / 8 fl oz water and simmer for 20-30 minutes or until very soft. Rub the cranberry mixture through a fine nylon sieve, then return the purée to the clean pan. Tie the spices in a muslin bag.

Stir the salt and vinegar into the cranberry purée, add the spice bag and simmer the mixture for 10- 15 minutes, stirring occasionally. Stir in the sugar, place over gentle heat and simmer the mixture until it starts to thicken. Stir frequently to prevent the sauce from sticking to the base of the pan.

Heat sufficient clean bottles to hold the ketchup; prepare vinegar-proof seals. When the mixture reaches the desired consistency, discard the spice bag and fill the hot bottles, leaving a 2cm / ¾ inch headspace. Seal the bottles immediately. Alternatively, allow the sauce to cool slightly, then fill the bottles (leaving a headspace) and sterilize at 88°C / 190°F for 30 minutes. Seal immediately. Label when cold. Store in a cool, dry place for at least two weeks before using.

CRESS VINEGAR

15g / ½oz cress seed
1 litre / 2 pints vinegar

Bruise the seed in a mortar, and put it into the vinegar, previously boiled and allowed to grow cold. Let it infuse for a fortnight, then strain and bottle for use.

CUCUMBER KETCHUP

Peel the cucumbers, slice them as thinly as possible into a basin, and sprinkle them liberally with salt. Let them remain closely covered until the following day, then strain the liquor from the cucumbers into a preserving-pan, add 5ml / 1 tsp peppercorns to each 600ml / 1 pint, and simmer gently for about half an hour. When cold, strain into bottles, seal tightly, and store in a cool, dry place. This ketchup imparts an agreeable flavour to sweetbreads, chicken mixtures and other delicate preparations.

CUCUMBER VINEGAR

Have ready 6 cucumbers and 1 litre / 2 pints vinegar.
To each 600ml / pint vinegar allow 2 shallots, 1 clove garlic,
5ml / 1 tsp white peppercorns, and 5ml / 1 tsp salt

Boil the vinegar, salt and peppercorns together for about 20 minutes, and allow the mixture to become quite cold. Slice the cucumbers without paring them into a wide necked bottle or jar, add the shallots and garlic, and the vinegar when cold. Let the preparation remain closely covered for fourteen days, then carefully strain off into smaller bottles, seal tightly, and store in a cool, dry place.

ESCAVEEKE SAUCE

1 litre / 2 pints white wine vinegar
finely grated rinds of 2 lemons
12 shallots
4 cloves garlic
30ml / 2 tbsp coriander seed
5ml / 1 tsp ground ginger
5ml / 1 tsp salt
5ml / 1 tsp cayenne

Pound all the dry ingredients well together, and put them into a preserving-pan. Boil the vinegar, and add it, boiling hot, to the pounded preparation. When quite cold, pour into small bottles, seal tightly, and store for use. It is important to keep this sauce in a cool, dry place.

FISH CONDIMENT SAUCE

Put 1 litre / 2 pints malt vinegar, 30ml / 2 tbsp walnut ketchup, 30ml / 2 tbsp soy, 25g / 1oz of cayenne, 1 clove of garlic, and 2 shallots sliced into a large bottle, and shake them daily for a fortnight. When ready, strain into small bottles, seal securely and store for use.

FRUIT SAUCE

450g / 1lb cooking apples
1 lemon, peeled and roughly chopped
450g / 1lb onions, roughly chopped
450g / 1lb tomatoes, roughly chopped
25g / 1oz salt
225g / 8oz sultanas
75g / 3oz sugar
25g / 1oz mixed spice
1 litre / 1¾ pints cider vinegar
25g / 1oz cornflour

Combine al the ingredients except the cornflour in a large saucepan or preserving pan. Bring to the boil, lower the heat and simmer until all the fruit and vegetables are thoroughly cooked.

In a cup, blend the cornflour to a paste with a little cold water.

Sieve the cooked mixture, return it to the pan and stir in the cornflour paste. Bring to the boil and boil for 5 minutes.

Fill hot bottles, leaving a 2cm / ¾ inch headspace. Seal the bottles immediately. Alternatively, allow the sauce to cool slightly, then fill the bottles (leaving a headspace) and sterilize at 88°C / 190°F for 30 minutes. Seal immediately. Label when cold.

GARLIC VINEGAR

(See Shallot Vinegar, page 171)

Use garlic in place of shallots.

HARVEY SAUCE

(For cold meat and salads)

1 litre / 2 pints good vinegar
3 anchovies
15ml / 1 tbsp soy sauce
142ml / ¼ pint walnut ketchup
1 finely chopped shallot
1 finely chopped clove garlic
7.5g / ¼oz cayenne
a few drops red food colouring

Cut each anchovy into 3 or 4 pieces, place them in a wide-necked bottle or jar, add the shallots, garlic and the rest of the ingredients, and cover closely. Let the jar stand for 14 days, during which time the contents must be either shaken or stirred at least once a day. At the end of this time strain into small bottles, seal them securely, and store the sauce in a cool, dry place until required.

HERB SAUCE

(For flavouring gravies and stews)

1 stick horseradish,
2 finely chopped shallots
few sprigs each winter savory, basil, marjoram,
thyme, tarragon
6 cloves
the thinly peeled rind and juice of 1 lemon
300ml / ½ pint vinegar
600ml / 1 pint water

Wash and scrape the horseradish, and remove the stalks of the herbs. Put all the ingredients together in a preserving-pan, simmer gently for about 20 minutes, then strain, and, when quite cold, pour into small bottles. Seal securely and store for use.

HORSERADISH VINEGAR

225g / 8 oz grated horseradish,
1 tbsp finely chopped shallots
5ml / 1 tsp salt
2.5ml / ½ tsp cayenne
2.3 litres / 4 pints good malt vinegar

Mix the horseradish, shallots, salt and cayenne together, boil the vinegar and pour it over them, cover closely, and allow the vessel to stand in a warm, but not hot, place for 10 days. Strain the vinegar into a preserving-pan, bring to boiling point, let it cool, then pour into small bottles, seal closely, and store in a cool, dry place.

INDIAN MUSTARD

100g / 4oz mustard
100g / 4oz flour
15g / ½oz salt
4 shallots chopped
142ml / ¼ pint vinegar
60ml / 4 tbsp mushroom ketchup
30ml / 2 tbsp anchovy sauce

Put the mustard, flour and salt into a basin, and mix them into a smooth paste with hot water. Boil the shallots with the vinegar, ketchup and anchovy sauce for about 10 minutes, then add the blended flour etc, and stir and simmer gently for 2 or 3 minutes. When quite cold pour the preparation into small bottles, seal them tightly, and store in a cool, dry place.

LEAMINGTON SAUCE

(For cold meat and fish)

Procure young green walnuts, pound them to a pulp, sprinkle liberally with salt, and let them remain for 3 days, stirring at frequent intervals. Strain the juice obtained, measure and for each 600 ml / 1 pint of walnut juice add 1.7 litres / 3 pints vinegar, 300ml / ½ pint Indian soy, 150ml / ¼ pint port wine, 25g / 1oz shallots, 7.5g / ¼oz garlic and 15g / ½oz cayenne, the garlic and shallots being previously pounded or finely chopped. Turn the whole into a large jar, cover closely for 3 weeks, then strain into small bottles, seal securely, and store for use.

LIVER, OR
MUSTAPHA KETCHUP

1 ox-liver
4.5 litres / 1 gallon water
25g / 1oz ginger
25g / 1oz allspice
50g / 2oz whole black pepper
900g / 2lb salt

Rub the salt well into a very fresh ox-liver, and place it in a vessel without crushing. Mince it up rather small, and boil in a gallon of water, closely covered until reduced to 3.3 litres / 6 pints. Strain through a sieve, put it aside until the following day, then add the pepper, allspice, and ginger, and boil slowly until reduced to 2.3 litres / 4 pints. When cold, bottle and keep well sealed.

MINT JELLY

1kg / 2¼lb green apples
1 small bunch mint
500ml / 18 fl oz distilled vinegar
sugar (see method)
20ml / 4 tsp finely chopped mint
green food colouring (optional)

Wash the apples, cut into quarters and put in a preserving pan with the small bunch of mint. Add 500ml / 18 fl oz water, bring to the boil, lower the heat and simmer until the apples are soft and pulpy. Add the vinegar, bring to the boil and boil for 5 minutes.

Strain through a scalded jelly bag and leave to drip for several hours or overnight. Measure the juice and return it to the clean pan. Add 800g / 1¾lb sugar for every 1 litre / 1¾ pints of juice.

Heat gently, stirring until the sugar has dissolved, then boil rapidly until close to setting point. Stir in the chopped mint, with colouring if used, and boil steadily until the setting point is reached. Remove from the heat, pot and cover immediately.

PRESSURE COOKER TIP

Combine the apples and 500ml / 18 fl oz water in the pressure cooker. Bring to 10lb pressure and cook for 5 minutes. Reduce the pressure slowly. Stir in the vinegar and boil in the open pressure cooker for 5 minutes. Mash the apples until well pulped, then strain as above and return to the clean cooker. Stir in sugar in the proportions above and add the bunch of mint, tied with string. Continue boiling until close to setting point. Remove mint bouquet and add chopped mint, with colouring, if used. Pot as above.

MINT VINEGAR

The mint for this purpose must be young and fresh. Pick the leaves from the stalks, and fill a bottle or jar with them. Cover with cold vinegar, cover closely, and let the mint infuse for 14 days. Then strain the liquor into small bottles, seal securely, and store for use.

MUSHROOM KETCHUP

Mushrooms intended for this purpose should be gathered on a dry day, otherwise the ketchup will not keep. Trim the tips of the stalks, but do not wash nor peel the mushrooms; simply rub any part not quite clean with a little salt. Place them in a large jar, sprinkling each layer liberally with salt. Let them remain for 3 days, stirring them at least 3 times daily. At the end of that time, cook them very gently either on the stove or in a cool oven, until the juice flows freely, then strain the mushrooms through a clean cloth, and drain well, but do not squeeze them.

Replace the liquor in the jar; to 1 litre / 2 pints mushroom liquor add 15g / ½oz allspice, 15g / ½oz ground ginger, 1.25ml / ¼ tsp pounded mace, and 1.25ml / ¼ tsp cayenne, place the jar in a saucepan of boiling water, and cook very gently for 3 hours. Strain 2 or 3 times through fine muslin when quite cold, pour into small bottles, seal securely and store for use.

MRS BEETON'S TIP

A dash of angostura bitters enhances the flavour of mushrooms.

PIQUANT SAUCE

(As condiment)

**Take 100 green walnuts, 2.3kg / 5lb fresh mushrooms,
and sufficient vinegar to cover
To each 600ml / 1 pint vinegar allow 5ml / 1 tsp soy, 6 shallots,
1 clove garlic, 2.5ml / ½ tsp ground ginger, 1.25ml / ¼ tsp allspice,
2 cloves, 1 blade mace, and 1.25ml / ¼ tsp cayenne**

Place the mushrooms and walnuts in separate bowls or pans, bruise them well with a pestle or potato masher, or, failing these, a heavy wooden spoon, and sprinkle them lightly with salt. Let them lie for a week. Turn and bruise them daily, then drain off the liquor, and squeeze the pulp as dry as possible. As a rule the quantity of juice thus obtained from the walnuts and mushrooms is nearly equal. Mix the two together, and boil gently until the scum, which must be carefully removed, ceases to rise.

Measure the liquid, return it to the pan with an equal quantity of vinegar, and shallots, garlic, ginger, mustard seed, allspice, cloves, mace, and cayenne in the above stated proportions. Simmer gently for about half an hour, skimming well meanwhile, then turn the liquid into an earthenware vessel, and add the soy. When quite cold, pour the sauce into small bottles, seal closely, and store in a dry, cool place until required for use.

PONTAC KETCHUP

**1 litre / 2 pints ripe elderberries
225g / 8oz anchovies
6 shallots
600ml / 1 pint vinegar
6 cloves
2 blades mace
about 25 peppercorns**

Remove the stalks, place the berries in a jar, cover them with vinegar, cook in a moderately hot oven for 3 hours, then strain and measure the vinegar. To each

1 litre / 2 pints add 225g / 8oz coarsely chopped anchovies, 25g / 1oz chopped shallots, 6 cloves, 2 blades mace, and 25 peppercorns. Simmer gently for about 1 hour, then strain and bottle for use.

QUIN'S SAUCE
(For roast duck, turkey, pork, etc)

Put 600ml / 1 pint of mushroom ketchup, 300ml / ½ pint of walnut pickle, 300ml / ½ pint of port wine, 150ml / ¼ pint of soy, 12 anchovies chopped, 12 shallots chopped, and 2.5ml / ½ tsp cayenne into a saucepan, simmer gently for about 15 minutes, and strain. When quite cold, bottle, seal securely and store for use.

RASPBERRY VINEGAR

1.4–1.8kg / 3–4lb raspberries
1.7–2.3 litres / 3–4 pints vinegar
sugar to taste

Cover the raspberries with vinegar, let them remain undisturbed for 4 days, then strain through a fine sieve, but do not press the fruit. Pour the vinegar over a fresh lot of raspberries and proceed as before. Repeat this process two or three times, taking care to drain each lot thoroughly. Measure the vinegar, to each 600ml / 1 pint add 100–150g / 4–5oz of sugar, simmer gently for 10 minutes, skimming well meanwhile. When quite cold, bottle for use. Or, put equal measures of raspberries and vinegar into a large jar, stir the mixture two or three times daily for 10 days, then strain off the vinegar. Measure it, adding about 50g / 2oz of sugar to each 600ml / 1 pint, boil up, skim well, and, when cold, bottle for use.

READING SAUCE

(For cold meat, etc)

1 litre / 2 pints walnut pickle
1 litre / 2 pints cold water
300ml / ½ pint soy sauce
40g / 1½oz shallots
15g / ½oz whole ginger bruised
15g / ½oz peppers
25g / 1oz mustard seed
15g / ½oz cayenne
7.5g / ¼oz bay leaves
15ml / 1 tbsp anchovy essence

Peel the shallots, chop them finely, place them in a heatproof jar with the liquor strained from the walnuts, and simmer gently until considerably reduced. In another heatproof jar put the water, soy, ginger, peppers, mustard seed, cayenne, and essence of anchovy, bring to the boil, and simmer gently for about 1 hour. Now mix the contents of the two jars together, and continue the slow cooking for about half an hour longer. Let the jar remain closely covered in a cool place until the following day, then add the bay leaves, replace the cover, and allow the jar to remain undisturbed for 7 days. At the end of this time, strain off the liquor into small bottles, and store for use.

SAUCE FOR STEAKS, CHOPS, etc

600ml / 1 pint mushroom ketchup or liquid from pickled walnuts
15g / ½oz pickled shallots
15g / ½oz grated horseradish
15g / ½oz allspice
25g / 1oz black pepper
25g / 1oz salt

Pound the shallots and horseradish until smooth in a mortar, add the rest of the ingredients, and let the whole stand closely covered for 14 days. Strain into small bottles, seal securely and store for use.

SHALLOT SAUCE

(As condiment)

600ml / 1 pint sherry
600ml / 1 pint vinegar
100g / 4oz shallots

Skin the shallots, chop them finely, and put them into a wide necked bottle. Pour over them the sherry and the vinegar, let them remain closely sealed for 14 days, then strain off the liquor into small bottles. Seal lightly, and store for use.

SHALLOT VINEGAR

Allow 1 litre / 2 pints good vinegar to
100g / 4oz shallots

Remove the skins, chop the shallots finely, and put them into a wide necked bottle. Pour in the vinegar, seal securely, and put the bottle aside for 10 days, during which time it must be shaken at least once a day. At the end of this time strain the vinegar through fine muslin, put it into small bottles, seal closely and store for use.

STORE SAUCE

(For cold meat, etc)

600ml / 1 pint mushroom ketchup
300ml / ½ pint walnut ketchup
150ml / ¼ pint port
12 anchovies
6 shallots
30ml / 2 tbsp cayenne

Pound the anchovies and shallots, or chop them finely; add them to the rest of the ingredients, and boil gently for about 1 hour. When cold, put the preparation into bottles, seal and store for use.

TAMARIND SAUCE

(For fruit salads or cold meat)

Place ripe tamarinds in layers in a heatproof dish sprinkling each layer slightly or liberally with sugar, according to taste. Cook in a cool oven until quite tender, then pass through a fine sieve, and when quite cold pour into small bottles, seal securely and store for use.

TARRAGON VINEGAR

Tarragon leaves intended for this purpose should be gathered on a dry day about the end of July, just before the plant begins to bloom. Remove the stalks, bruise the leaves slightly, put them into a wide-necked bottle, and cover them with vinegar. Cover closely so as to completely exclude the air, and let the bottle stand in a cool, dry place for 7 or 8 weeks. Now strain the liquid through fine muslin until it is quite clear, put it into small bottles, seal tightly, and store them in a cool, dry place.

TOMATO KETCHUP

900g / 2lb ripe tomatoes
2 onions
4 green pepper pods
2 tbsp salt
10ml / 2 tsp Demerara sugar
15ml / 1 tbsp ground ginger
2.5ml / ½ tsp mustard
1 ground nutmeg
2.2 litres / 4 pints vinegar

Peel and crush the tomatoes, and peel and slice the onions; chop the green pepper pods finely. Put these with all the other ingredients, carefully mixed, in a preserving-pan, and boil for about 2 hours, stirring frequently. Rub all through a sieve, bottle whilst hot, and store in a cool, dry place.

MRS BEETON'S TIP

Bottles of ketchup for keeping should be wrapped in foil. This helps to keep the colour bright.

TOMATO SAUCE I

Bake the tomatoes in a slow oven until tender, rub them through a fine sieve, and measure the pulp. To each 1 litre / 2 pints of pulp allow 600ml / 1 pint of chilli vinegar, 150ml / ¼ pint of soy, 15ml / 1 tbsp anchovy essence, 2 finely chopped shallots, 1 finely chopped clove of garlic and salt to taste. Place all the ingredients in a preserving-pan, simmer until the shallots and garlic are quite tender, and pass the whole through a fine sieve. Store in airtight bottles.

TOMATO SAUCE II

12 large tomatoes
2 Spanish onions
25g / 1oz salt
2.5ml / ½ tsp cayenne
600ml / 1 pint vinegar

Peel the onions, slice them thinly, place them in a csserole dish with the tomatoes, and cook in a slow oven until tender. Pass the pulp through a fine sieve, put it into a preserving-pan with the vinegar, salt and cayenne, and simmer gently for about 10 minutes. Store for use in small airtight bottles.

TOMATO VINEGAR

18 sound tomatoes
75–100g / 3–4oz salt
150ml / ¼ pint mustard seeds
mace, cloves and nutmeg
1 litre / 2 pints good vinegar

Cut each tomato into quarters, but without separating it at the bottom. Place in a large heat-proof dish, sprinkling each layer with salt, and cook in a very slow oven for 12 hours. Add the mustard seeds and spices to taste, boil and add the vinegar, and cover closely. Leave the dish in a warm place for 5–6 days, and either stir or shake it several times daily. When ready, strain into small bottles, seal them securely and store for use.

VINEGAR, SPICED

1 litre / 2 pints good vinegar
50g / 2oz black peppercorns
25g / 1oz whole ginger
15g / ½oz salt
15g / ½oz allspice
25g / 1oz finely chopped shallots
2 cloves garlic bruised
2 bay leaves

Pound or crush the peppercorns, ginger and allspice, put all into a jar, add the rest of the ingredients, and cover closely. Let the jar remain in a warm place for 1 week, then place it in a saucepan containing boiling water, and cook gently for about 1 hour. When cold, cover closely, and store for use.

MRS BEETON'S TIP

The choice of which vinegar to use in sauce making is a matter of personal taste. Where keeping the true colour of the prime ingredient is important, as when making tomato ketchup, distilled white vinegar is generally used, but for other sauces malt vinegar is often preferred. Cider vinegar is particularly good with spicy fruit sauces.

WALNUT KETCHUP

100 green walnuts
2.2 litres / 4 pints good vinegar
75g / 3oz salt
100g / 4oz anchovies
12 finely chopped shallots
½ stick finely grated horseradish
2.5ml / ½ tsp each mace, nutmeg, ground ginger,
ground cloves and pepper
300ml / ½ pint port

The walnuts must be very young and tender. Bruise them slightly, put them into a jar with the salt and vinegar, and let them remain for 8 days, stirring them daily. Drain the liquor from them into a preserving-pan, add to it the rest of the ingredients, simmer very gently for about 40 minutes, and when quite cold, strain the preparation into small bottles. Seal them closely and store in a cool, dry place.

WORCESTER SAUCE

(For cold meat or fish)

Put 1 litre / 2 pints best malt vinegar, 90ml / 6 tbsp walnut ketchup, 75ml / 5 tbsp anchovy essence, 60ml / 4 tbsp soy, 2.5 ml / ½ tsp cayenne, 4 very finely chopped shallots, and salt to taste into a large bottle, and seal it closely. Shake it well three or four times daily for about 14 days, then strain the sauce into small bottles, seal them tightly and store in a cool, dry place.

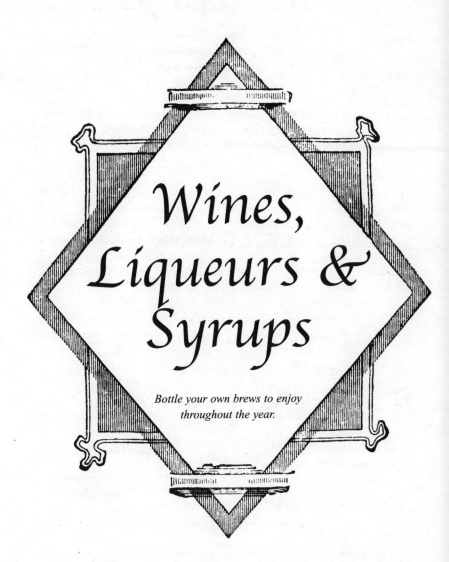

Wines, Liqueurs & Syrups

Bottle your own brews to enjoy throughout the year.

ANISE LIQUEUR

1 litres / 2 pints good brandy
25g / 1oz aniseed
450g / 1lb granulated sugar
600ml / 1 pint water

Put the aniseed into the brandy, and let it stand, closely corked, for a fortnight, shaking it occasionally; boil the sugar and water to a syrup, and strain the brandy into it. When cool, pour into dry, clean bottles, cork securely, and store for use.

APPLE WINE

Put 23 litres / 5 gallons of good cider into a cask it will about three quarters fill, add 4.5kg / 10lb of granulated sugar, and stir occasionally with a wooden spoon until the sugar is quite dissolved; at the end of 48 hours put in the bung, and place a small vent peg near the top of the cask. Allow the cask to remain for 12 months in a cool, dry place, when the wine will be ready for use.

APRICOT WINE

900g / 2lb sound but not overripe apricots
450g / 1lb granulated sugar
600ml / 1 pint white wine
14 litres / 3 gallons water
15ml / 1 tbsp compressed yeast,
or 15ml / 1 tbsp good brewers' yeast

Remove the stones of the fruit, take out the kernels, and cut each apricot into 6 or 8 pieces. Put them into a preserving-pan with the water, sugar, and about half the kernels, and simmer very gently for about 1 hour. Turn the whole into an earthenware vessel, let it remain undisturbed until cool, then stir in the yeast; if compressed yeast is used it must previously be mixed smoothly with a little warm water. Cover the vessel with a cloth, let it remain undisturbed for 3 days, then strain the liquid into a clean, dry cask, add the white wine, and bung lightly. At the end of 6 months draw off the wine into bottles, cork them closely, store in a cool, dry place for about 12 months, and the wine will then be ready for use.

ARRACK LIQUEUR

**To 1 litre / 2 pints Arrack allow 1 litre / 2 pints water,
450g / 1lb sugar crystals, and the rind of ½ a lemon**

Remove the outer part of the lemon-rind as thinly as possible, add it and the sugar crystals to the water, and boil gently until a moderately thick syrup is formed. When cold, strain and add it to the Arrack, bottle, cork securely and store for use.

ARRACK This spirit is produced by fermenting the juice of the cocoa and other palms; it is extensively used in the East.

BLACKCURRANT LIQUEUR

**450g / 1lb blackcurrants
350g / 12oz brown sugar crystals
900ml / 1½ pints gin**

Strip the fruit from the stalks, put it into a wide-necked bottle, add the sugar crystals crushed to a fine powder, and pour in the gin. Let it stand for 2 months, then strain until it is quite clear, rack off into bottles, cork and store in a cool, dry place until required.

BLACKCURRANT WINE

Have ready some ripe blackcurrants
To each 600ml / 1 pint of juice obtained add 600ml / 1 pint cold water,
450g / 1lb preserving sugar and a good glass best brandy

Take away the stalks, put the currants into an earthenware bowl, bruise well
with a wooden spoon, then drain off the juice and put it aside. Add the water to
the berries, stir them frequently for 2 or 3 hours, then strain the liquid and mix
it with the juice. Add the sugar, and as soon as it is dissolved turn the whole into
a cask. When fermentation has ceased rack off the liquid in to a smaller cask,
add the brandy, bung closely, and let it remain for at least 12 months in a warm
place. At the end of this time drain the wine off carefully into dry bottles, cork
them tightly and store in a dry, moderately warm place.

CARAWAY LIQUEUR

25g / 1oz caraway seeds
225g / ½ lb granulated sugar
1 litre / 2 pints brandy
300ml / ½ pint water

Boil the sugar and water to thin syrup, pour it, quite boiling, over the caraway
seeds, let it cool slightly, and add the brandy. When quite cold pour the whole
into a bottle, cork securely, allow it to stand for 10 days, then strain into small
bottles, cork them tightly, and store in a cool, dry place until required.

CHERRY BOUNCE

Remove the stones, place the fruit in a large pan, and stand the pan over a saucepan containing boiling water. Cook gently until all the juice is extracted, strain it, and measure it into a preserving-pan. To each gallon of juice add 1.8kg / 4lb of sugar, 2.5ml / ½ tsp ground mace, 1.25ml / ¼ tsp ground allspice, 1 litre / 2 pints brandy, and 1 litre / 2 pints rum, and simmer the ingredients until the scum ceases to rise. When cold bottle for use.

CHERRY BRANDY

To each 450g / 1lb sound Morello cherries allow 75g / 3oz brown sugar crystals, 12 apricot, peach, or plum kernels, 2.5ml / ½ tsp bitter almond essence, 5mm / ¼ inch cinnamon, and good French brandy to cover

Cut off the stalks, leaving them about ½ inch in length, wipe the cherries with a soft cloth, and prick them well with a coarse darning needle; half fill some wide-necked bottles with the prepared fruit; to each one add sugar crystals, etc, in the above stated proportions, and fill the bottles with brandy. Cork closely and keep for at least 3 months before using. Shake the bottle well at intervals.

CHERRY LIQUEUR

Remove the stalks and stones from 450g / 1lb of Morello cherries and 450g / 1lb of black cherries, crush the stones and cherries, put them into a bottle with 225g / ½ lb granulated or good preserving sugar, 7.5g / ¼ oz stick of cinnamon, 12 cloves, and pour over them brandy. Cork closely, let it stand for 14 days, then strain into small bottles, cork securely, and store in a cool dry place.

CHERRY WINE I

Place the cherries, preferably small black ones, on a large dish and bruise them well with a large wooden spoon. Allow them to remain until the following day, then drain them well on a sieve, and measure the juice into a bowl. To each 1 litre / 2 pints of juice add 225g / 8oz good preserving sugar, cover the vessel, let it stand for 24 hours, and strain the liquor into a clean, dry cask. Bung closely, but provide the upper part of the cask with a vent-peg; let it remain undisturbed for about 6 months, then drain off into bottles. Cork closely, and store in a cool, dry place.

CHERRY WINE II

Stone the cherries, which should be nice and ripe, put them into a large pan, place over a saucepan of boiling water, and cook gently until the juice is all extracted. Then strain and measure the juice into a preserving-pan. To each 1 litre / 2 pints of juice allow 225g / 8oz granulated sugar, a pinch each of ground mace, cloves and allspice, 300ml / ½ pint of brandy and 300ml / ½ pint of rum. Add sugar and the above ingredients, and boil and skim until clear. Let it cool, add the spirits, pour into bottles, and cork them closely.

CITRON LIQUEUR

Remove the rinds of 4 lemons as thinly as possible, pour over them 600ml / 1 pint of spirits of wine or gin, cover and put aside for 10 days. On the tenth day make 600ml / 1 pint of syrup, add the strained juice of 4 lemons and, when cold, strain and mix in the spirits of wine or gin. Bottle, cork securely and store for use.

CLARY WINE

To each 4.5 litres / gallon water allow 1.4kg / 3lb preserving sugar,
30ml / 2 tbsp brewers' yeast moistened with water,
1 litre / 2 pints clary flowers and tops and
300ml / ½ pint good brandy

Dissolve the sugar in the water, bring to the boil, simmer gently for about 10 minutes, skimming meanwhile, and when cool pour it into a clean dry cask. Add a little of the warm syrup to the yeast, and when it is working well stir it together with the clary flowers and tops, into the rest of the syrup. Stir vigorously twice daily for 5 days, and bung closely as soon as fermentation ceases. Let it remain undisturbed for 4 months, then drain it carefully from the sediment; add the brandy, pour into bottles, and cork securely. After being stored for about 6 months in a cool, dry place, it will be ready for use.

CLOVE LIQUEUR

100g / ¼lb cloves
100g / ¼lb coriander seed
225g / ¼lb granulated sugar
2 dozen large black cherries
1 litre / 2 pints gin or brandy

Remove the stalks and stones from the cherries, bruise the stones, also the cloves and coriander seed. Put the whole into a wide-necked bottle, add the sugar, pour in the brandy and cover closely for 1 month. When ready, strain the liquid into small bottles, cover closely, and store for use.

COWSLIP WINE

4.4 litres / 8 pints cowslip flowers
4.4 litres / 8 pints water
1.4kg / 3lb granulated sugar
finely grated rind and juice of 1 orange and 1 lemon
30ml / 2 tbsp brewers' yeast, or 7.5g / ¼oz
compressed yeast moistened with water
150ml / ¼ pint brandy, if liked

Boil the sugar and water together for about half an hour, skimming when necessary, and pour, quite boiling, over the rinds and strained juice of the orange and
lemon. Let it cool, then stir in the yeast and cowslip flowers, cover with a cloth,
and allow it to remain undisturbed for 48 hours. Turn the whole into a clean dry
cask, add the brandy, bung closely, let it remain thus for 8 weeks, then draw it
off into bottles. Cork securely, store in a cool, dry place for 3 or 4 weeks, and
it will then be ready for use.

CURAÇAO

1 litre / 2 pints brandy
450g / 1lb granulated sugar
300ml / ½ pint cold water
300ml / ½ pint boiling water
50g / 2oz very thinly pared orange rind

Put the orange rinds into a jar, pour over them the boiling water; when cool, add
the brandy. Cover closely, let the liquid stand for 10 days in a moderately warm
place, and stir it two or three times daily. On the tenth day boil the sugar and
cold water together until reduced to a thick syrup, let this become quite cold,
then add to it the liquid from the jar previously strained through flannel or fine
muslin until clear. Pour into small bottles, cork tightly, and store.

CURRANT AND RASPBERRY WINE

To 23 litres / 5 gallons redcurrant juice allow 600ml / 1 pint raspberry juice, 45 litres / 10 gallons water and 4.5kg / 10lb granulated sugar or preserving sugar

Extract the juice as directed in the two following recipes. Add to it the water and sugar, stir until the latter is dissolved, then turn the whole into a cask, and bung closely, but provide the top of the cask with a vent-peg. As soon as fermentation ceases, tighten the vent-peg, and let the cask remain undisturbed in a moderately warm place for 12 months. At the end of this time rack off into dry bottles, cork them closely and store. The wine should be ready for use in about 3 months.

DAMSON GIN

(See Sloe Gin, page 200)

DAMSON WINE

**To each 4.5 litres / gallon damsons add 4.5 litres / 1 gallon boiling water
To each 4.5 litres / gallon liquor obtained from these add
1.8kg / 4lb granulated sugar and 300ml / ½ pint best brandy**

Remove the stalks, put the fruit into an earthenware bowl, pour in the boiling water, and cover with a cloth. Stir the liquid three or four times daily for 4 days, then add the sugar and brandy, and when the former is dissolved turn the whole into a clean dry cask. Cover the bung-hole with a cloth, folded into several thicknesses, until fermentation ceases, then bung tightly, and allow the cask to remain undisturbed for 12 months in a moderately warm place. At the end of this time it should be racked off into bottles. The wine may be used at once, but if well corked and stored in a dry place it may be kept for years.

DANDELION WINE

4.4 litres / 8 pints dandelion flowers
4.4 litres / 8 pints boiling water
1.4kg / 3lb granulated sugar
2.5 cm / 1 inch whole ginger
1 lemon
thinly pared rind of 1 orange
15ml / 1 tbsp brewers' yeast, or 7.5g / ¼oz compressed
yeast moistened with water

Put the petals of the flowers into a bowl, pour over them the boiling water, let the bowl remain covered for 3 days, meanwhile stirring it well and frequently. Strain the liquid into a preserving-pan, add the rinds of the orange and lemon, both of which should be pared off in thin fine strips, the sugar, ginger, and the lemon previously stripped of its white pith and thinly sliced. Boil gently for about half an hour, and when cool add the yeast spread on a piece of toast. Allow it to stand for 2 days, then turn it into a cask, keep it well bunged down for 8 or 9 weeks, and bottle the wine for use.

ELDERBERRY WINE

3.2kg / 7lb elderberries
14 litres / 3 gallons water

Strip the berries from the stalks, pour the water, quite boiling, over them, let them stand for 24 hours, then bruise well and drain through a fine sieve or jelly-bag. Measure the juice obtained, and to each 4.5 litres / gallon of liquid allow 1.4kg / 3lb granulated sugar, 450g / 1lb of raisins, 15g / ½ oz of ground ginger, 6 cloves, 150ml / ¼ pint of brandy, 2.5ml / ½ tsp brewers' yeast. Put the juice into a preserving-pan with sugar, raisins, ginger, and cloves, boil gently for about 1 hour, and skim when necessary. Let the liquid stand until milk-warm, then stir in the yeast and turn the whole into a clean, dry cask. Cover the bung-hole with a folded cloth, let the cask remain undisturbed for 14 days, then stir in the brandy and bung tightly. In about 6 months the wine may be drawn off into bottles, tightly corked and stored for use.

FOUR-FRUIT LIQUEUR

350g / 12oz strawberries
350g / 12oz Kentish cherries
225g / ½lb raspberries
225g / ½lb blackcurrants

Strip the fruit from the stalks, put it into a jar, stand the latter in a saucepan of boiling water, and cook gently for about 1 hour. Strain the juice through a jelly-bag, being careful not to press the pulp, and to each 600ml / 1 pint of strained juice add 300ml / ½ pint of French brandy, 75g / 3oz of granulated sugar, and half the cherry kernels. Cover closely, let the liqueur stand for 3 days, then strain it into small bottles and cork them securely.

GINGER BRANDY

50g / 2oz Jamaica ginger
1 litre / 2 pints brandy
300ml / ½ pint water
450g / 1lb sugar
50g / 2oz juniper berries (mixed black and white)

Crush finely the ginger and juniper berries, put them into a wide-necked bottle, and pour in the brandy. Cork securely, let the bottle stand in a warm place for 3 days, shaking it three or four times daily. On the third day boil the sugar and water to a thick syrup, and when cool add to it the brandy, which must previously be strained through fine muslin or filtering paper until quite clear. When quite cold pour into clean, dry bottles, cork securely, and store in a cool place until required for use.

GINGER WINE I

14 litres / 3 gallons cold water
4kg / 9lb granulated sugar
100g / ¼lb fresh ginger, bruised
100g / ¼lb raisins
the strained juice and finely-pared rinds of 4 lemons
15ml / 1 tbsp brewers' yeast

Stone and halve the raisins, put them into a large preserving-pan with the water, sugar and ginger bruised; boil for about 1 hour, skimming frequently. Turn the whole into a large earthenware bowl, allow the liquid to stand until milk-warm, then stir in the yeast. On the following day put the preparation into a clean, dry cask, add the lemon juice, and bung lightly. Stir the wine every day for a fortnight, then tighten the bung. Let the wine remain undisturbed for 3 or 4 months, when it may be bottled for use.

GINGER WINE II

27 litres / 6 gallons water
450g / 1lb granulated sugar
175g / 6oz whole ginger bruised
1.8kg / 4lb Muscatel raisins
1.8kg / 4lb Valencia raisins
15g / ½oz isinglass
6 lemons
30ml / 2 tbsp yeast
600ml / 1 pint brandy

Remove the peel of the lemons as thinly as possible, and boil it with the water, sugar and ginger for about half an hour. Meanwhile stone and halve the raisins, put them into an earthenware bowl, pour the liquid over them when nearly cold, add the lemon juice and yeast. Stir it every day for a fortnight, then add the isinglass previously dissolved in a little warm water, and drain into a clean, dry cask. Let the wine remain closely bunged for about 3 months, then bottle for use.

GOOSEBERRY WINE I

To each 450g / 1lb firm green gooseberries
allow 1 litre / 2 pints cold water
To each 4.5 litres / gallon juice obtained from the
fruit allow 1.4 kg / 3 lb granulated sugar,
300ml / ½ pint gin and 20g / ¾oz isinglass

Top and tail the gooseberries, bruise them thoroughly, pour over them the cold water, and let them stand for about 4 days, stirring frequently. Strain through a jelly-bag or fine sieve, dissolve the sugar in the liquid, add the gin and isinglass dissolved in a little warm water, and pour the whole into a cask. Bung loosely until fermentation has ceased, then tighten the bung, and let the cask remain undisturbed for at least 6 months. At the end of this time the wine may be bottled, but it will not be ready for use for at least 12 months.

GOOSEBERRY WINE II

9kg / 20lb firm green gooseberries
14 litres / 3 gallons hot water
7kg / 15lb granulated sugar
40g / 1½oz cream of tartar

Top and tail the gooseberries, put them into an earthenware bowl and pour over them the hot water. Let them soak for 24 hours, then bruise them well and drain the juice through a fine sieve or jelly bag. Replace the skins in the vessel in which they were soaked, cover them with boiling water, stir and bruise well so as to extract the juice completely, then strain through the sieve or bag.

Mix this preparation with the juice, add the sugar, and boiling water to increase the liquid to 23 litres / 5 gallons. Replace in the bowl, stir in the cream of tartar, cover with a heavy cloth, and allow the vessel to stand in a moderately warm place for 2 days. Now strain the liquid into a small cask, cover the bung-hole with a folded cloth until fermentation ceases – which may be known by the cessation of the hissing noise – then bung closely, but provide the top of the cask with a vent-peg.

Make this wine in the beginning of June, before the berries ripen; let it remain undisturbed until December, then drain it off carefully into a clean cask. In March or April, or when the gooseberry bushes begin to blossom, the wine must be bottled and tightly corked. To ensure its being clear and effervescing, the wine must be bottled at the right time.

GRAPE WINE

**Have ready some sound, not overripe grapes and to each
450g / 1lb allow 1 litre / 2 pints cold water**

Strip the grapes from the stalks, put them into an earthenware bowl, and bruise them well. Pour over them the water, let them stand for 3 days, stirring frequently, then strain through a jelly-bag or fine sieve. To each 4.5 litres / gallon of liquid obtained from the grapes allow 1.4kg / 3 lb of granulated sugar, 150ml / ¼ pint of French brandy, and about 7.5g / ¼ oz of isinglass. Dissolve the sugar in the liquid, then pour the whole into a cask. Bung lightly for a few days until fermentation subsides, then add the isinglass dissolved in a little warm water, and the brandy, and tighten the bung. Let the cask remain undisturbed for 6 months, then rack the wine off into bottles, cork and seal them securely, and keep for at least a year before using.

HAWTHORN LIQUEUR

**Have ready some white hawthorn blossoms and sufficient
good brandy to cover**

Gather the blossoms on a dry day, put them into wide-necked bottles, shaking, but not pressing, them down. Fill the bottles with brandy, cork them securely, let them remain thus for 4 months, then strain the liqueur into small bottles and cork tightly. This liqueur is used chiefly for flavouring creams, custards, etc.

LEMON FLIP

150ml / ¼ pint lemon juice
rind 2 lemons
150–175g / 5–6oz caster sugar
4 eggs
600ml / 1 pint boiling water
about 150ml / ¼ pint sherry

Peel the rind off 2 lemons in the thinnest possible strips. Put them into a jug with the sugar, add the boiling water, and let it stand until cold. Now stir in the well-beaten eggs, the strained lemon juice and the sherry, strain through a fine strainer, and use as required. It will not keep for any length of time.

LEMON GIN
(See Citron Liqueur, page 183)

LEMON WINE

10 lemons
1.8kg / 4lb granulated sugar
4.4 litres / 8 pints boiling water
15ml / 1 tbsp brewers' yeast

Remove the rinds of 5 lemons in thin fine strips, and place them in a wooden tub or earthenware bowl. Boil the sugar and water together for about half an hour, then pour the syrup over the lemon-peel. When cool add the strained juice of the 10 lemons, stir in the yeast, and let the vessel stand for 48 hours. At the end of this time strain into a cask, which the wine must quite fill, bung loosely until fermentation ceases, then tighten the bung, and allow the cask to remain undisturbed for about 6 months before racking the wine off into bottles.

NOYEAU I

(Imitation)

125g / 5oz almonds
450g / 1lb granulated sugar
1 litre / 2 pints brandy or gin
30ml / 2 tbsp honey
1.25ml / ¼ tsp bitter almond essence

Blanch the almonds, pound them well in a mortar, or chop them very finely, put them into a clean wide-necked bottle or jar, pour into them the spirit, and cover closely. Keep the jar in a moderately cool place for 3 days, shaking frequently, then add the honey and sugar, and stir occasionally until they are dissolved. Strain through very fine muslin into small bottles, and seal them securely. Store in a cool, dry place. Apricot, nectarine, or peach kernels can be used instead of the almonds.

NOYEAU II

(Imitation)

1.7 litres / 3 pints French brandy
300 ml / ½ pint boiling milk
675g / 1½ lb granulated sugar
100g / 4oz almonds, blanched
3.5g / ⅛ oz stick cinnamon and 1 lemon
1.25ml / ¼ tsp bitter almond essence

Remove the rind of the lemon as thinly as possible, put it into a wide-necked bottle, add the sugar, cinnamon, almonds, and the juice of ½ the lemon. Shake occasionally until the sugar is dissolved, then add the milk, quite boiling, and when cold add the brandy and cover closely. Shake the bottle three or four times a day for 3 weeks, then strain into small bottles, seal securely, and store for use.

ORANGE BRANDY

**To 2.2 litres / 4 pints French brandy allow 450ml / ¾ pint
orange juice, the rind of 6 oranges and
550g / 1¼lb granulated sugar**

Remove the rinds of 6 oranges as thinly as possible, mix the strained orange juice and brandy together, add the prepared rinds and sugar, and turn the whole into a wide-necked bottle. Seal closely, shake it two or three times daily for about 30 days, then strain into small bottles, and store in a cool place.

ORANGE LIQUEUR

**peel of 3 Seville oranges
900ml / 1½ pints gin
450g / 1lb granulated sugar
150ml / ¼ pint water
pinch saffron**

Remove the rinds of the oranges in fine strips, and put them into a wide-necked bottle or jar, with the saffron and gin. Boil the sugar and water to a thick syrup; when cool add it to the contents of the bottle. Cover closely and let it remain in a moderately warm place for a month. Then strain into small bottles, seal securely, and store in a cool cellar.

ORANGE WINE

**To the juice of 50 Seville oranges allow 7kg / 15lb granulated sugar,
18 litres / 4 gallons water, the whites and shells 3 eggs, 600ml / 1 pint
best French brandy and about 45ml / 3 tbsp brewers' yeast**

Dissolve the sugar in the water, add the whites and crushed shells of the eggs,
bring to the boil, and simmer gently for about 20 minutes. Let it stand until
nearly cold, then strain through a jelly-bag, add the strained orange juice and
yeast and leave the vessel covered for 24 hours. Pour into a cask, bung loosely
until fermentation subsides, then tighten the bung, and allow the cask to remain
undisturbed for 3 months. At the end of this time rack it off into another cask,
add the brandy, let it remain closely bunged for 12 months, then bottle and use
as required.

PARSNIP WINE

**To 1.8kg / 4lb parsnips allow 1.4kg / 3lb Demerara sugar,
7.5g / ¼ oz mild hops, 15ml / 1 tbsp fresh yeast, 1 slice
toasted bread, and 4.4 litres / 8 pints boiling water**

Boil the parsnips gently in the water for about 15 minutes, add the hops, and
cook for about 10 minutes longer. Strain, add the sugar, let the liquid become
lukewarm, and put in the toast spread with the yeast. Let it ferment for 36 hours,
then turn it into a cask, which it should fill. As soon as fermentation ceases,
strain into small bottles, cork securely, and store in a cool, dry place for at least
1 month before using.

RAISIN WINE I

**To each 450g / 1lb raisins allow 4.5 litres / 1 gallon cold water,
900g / 2lb good preserving sugar and 15ml / 1 tbsp yeast**

Strip the raisins from the stalks, put them into a large preserving-pan with the
water, simmer gently for about 1 hour, then rub them through a sieve. Dissolve

the sugar in the liquid, and add the raisin pulp and the yeast, let the vessel stand covered for 3 days, then strain the liquid into a cask. Bung loosely until fermentation ceases, then tighten the bung, and allow the cask to stand for at least 12 months before racking the wine off into bottles.

RAISIN WINE II

16lb / 7kg raisins
9 litres / 2 gallons water

Strip the raisins from the stalks, put them into an earthenware bowl, pour over the water, and let them remain covered for 4 weeks, stirring daily. At the end of this time strain the liquid into a cask which it will quite fill, bung loosely until fermentation subsides, then tighten the bung, and allow the cask to remain undisturbed for 12 months. Now rack it off carefully into another cask, straining the liquid near the bottom of the cask repeatedly until quite clear, let it stand for at least 2 years, and then bottle for use.

RAISIN WINE WITH CIDER

36 litres / 8 gallons good cider
6.8kg / 15lb Malaga raisins
1 bottle good French brandy
75g / 3oz sugar crystals
rind and juice of 3 or 4 lemons

Strip the raisins from the stalks, halve them, put them into a 40-litre / 9-gallon cask, and pour over them the cider. Bung lightly for 5 or 6 days, then tighten the bung and let the cask stand for 6 months. Strain into another cask, passing the liquid near the bottom repeatedly through a jelly-bag or fine muslin until quite clear, add the brandy, the sugar crystals crushed to a powder, and the finely-pared rind and strained juice of the lemons. Keep the wine well bunged for 2 years, then bottle, cork and seal securely, store it in a cool, dry place for one year longer, when it will be ready for use.

RASPBERRY AND REDCURRANT WINE

7 litres / 3 pints raspberries
4.5 litres / 1 gallon redcurrants
11 litres / 20 pints water
4.5kg / 10lb preserving sugar
600ml / 1 pint French brandy

Strip the redcurrants from the stalks, put them into a large earthenware bowl, and pour over the water (which must have previously boiled and allowed to become quite cold). On the following day crush the redcurrants, add the raspberries, and allow the whole to stand until the following day. Strain the liquid through a jelly-bag or fine sieve, and drain the fruit thoroughly, but do not squeeze it. Stir in the sugar, and when quite dissolved turn the wine into a clean, dry cask. Bung loosely until fermentation has entirely subsided, then tighten the bung, and allow the cask to remain undisturbed for 3 months. At the end of this time rack the wine off carefully, straining that near the bottom of the cask repeatedly until quite clear. Scald and drain the cask, replace the wine, add the brandy, bung lightly, let it remain 2 months longer in the cask, and then bottle.

RASPBERRY BRANDY

To 600ml / 1 pint ripe raspberries allow 1 litre / 2 pints
French brandy, 100g / ¼ lb granulated sugar and about 30ml /
2 tbsp cold water

Put the raspberries into a wide-necked bottle, pour the brandy over them, cork the bottle tightly, and let it stand in a moderately warm place for 14 days. Have ready a thick syrup, made by boiling together the sugar and water until the right consistency is obtained. Strain the liquor from the bottle repeatedly until quite clear, then mix it with the syrup, and pour the whole into small bottles. Seal them securely, and store for use.

RASPBERRY GIN

**To 1 litre / 2 pints ripe raspberries add 1 litre / 2 pints gin
and 450g / 1lb sugar crystals**

Pound the sugar crystals into small pieces, put it in a jar with the raspberries
and gin, cover closely, and let it remain thus for 12 months, shaking it daily for
three or four weeks. At the end of the time strain or filter until clear, and bottle
for use.

RASPBERRY WINE

**To 11 litres / 20 pints ripe raspberries allow 11 litres / 20 pints boiled
water, 2.7kg / 6lb preserving sugar, 30ml / 2 tbsp brewers' yeast,
600ml / 1 pint French brandy and 7.5g / ¼oz isinglass**

Prepare the fruit in the usual way, put into an earthenware or wooden vessel,
bruise well with a heavy wooden spoon and add the cold water. Let them stand
until the following day, stirring frequently. Strain the liquid through a jelly-bag
or fine sieve and drain the fruit thoroughly, but avoid squeezing it. Measure the
liquid; to each 1 litre / 2 pints add 450g / 1lb granulated sugar; stir occasionally
until dissolved, then pour into a cask. Bung loosely for several days until
fermentation ceases, then tighten the bung. Leave thus for 3 months, then bottle
for use.

RATAFIA

100g / 4oz cherry kernels, preferably Morello cherries
25g / 1oz apricot or peach kernels
1 bottle good brandy
225g / ½ lb sugar crystals
150ml / ¼ pint cold water

Pound the kernels until smooth, moistening them from time to time with a few drops of brandy. Put them with the remainder of the brandy into a wide-necked bottle, cover closely and shake two or three times daily for 6 weeks. Strain the liqueur first through fine muslin and then through filtering paper, add the sugar crystals finely powdered and dissolved in cold water, bottle, cork tightly and store for use.

REDCURRANT WINE

Procure some ripe red currants
To each 4.5 litres / gallon of fruit allow 7 litres / 1½ gallons cold water,
2.25kg / 5lb either granulated sugar or preserving sugar
and 300ml / ½ pint good brandy

Remove the stalks from the currants, place in an earthenware bowl, bruise well with a wooden spoon, and drain off the juice. Put the juice aside, add the water to the berries and leave for 2 or 3 hours, stirring occasionally. Then strain the liquid from the berries into the juice, add three quarters of the sugar, stir occasionally until dissolved and pour the whole into a cask, filling it three parts full. Bung closely, but place a vent-peg near the top of the cask, and leave for 1 month in a uniform temperature of about 18°C / 65°F. Dissolve the remaining sugar in the smallest possible quantity of warm water, mix well with the contents of the cask, replace the bung and leave undisturbed for 6 weeks longer. Now drain off the wine into a clean, dry cask, add the brandy, let the cask stand for about 6 months in a dry, warm place, then bottle and cork tightly. The wine may be used at once, but will be better if kept for 12 months at least.

Note: See also recipes for Currant and Raspberry Wine, page 185, and Blackcurrant Wine, page 180.

RHUBARB WINE

11kg / 25lb rhubarb
23 litres / 5 gallons water
25g / 1oz isinglass

Wipe the rhubarb with a damp cloth, and cut it into short lengths, leaving on the peel. Put it into an earthenware bowl, crush it thoroughly and pour over it the water. Let it remain covered for 10 days, stirring it daily; then strain and measure the liquor into another vessel. To each 4.5 litres / gallon of liquid add 1.4kg / 3lb of preserving sugar and the juice and very thinly pared rind of 1 lemon, and stir occasionally until the sugar is dissolved. Now put it into a cask, and add the isinglass dissolved in a little warm water; cover the bung-hole with a folded cloth for 10 days, then bung securely, and allow it to remain undisturbed for 12 months. At the end of this time rack off into bottles and use.

SHRUB

To 2.25 litres / 4 pints rum allow 450ml / ¾ pint orange
juice, 300ml / ½ pint lemon juice, the peel of 2 lemons,
900g / 2lb granulated sugar and 1.4 litres / 2½ pints water

Slice the lemon peel very thinly, and put it, with the fruit juice and spirit, in a large covered jar. Let it stand for a day, then pour over it the water in which the sugar has been dissolved, take out the lemon peel, and leave it for 12 days before using.

SLOE GIN

Half fill clean, dry wine bottles with sloes previously pricked with a fine skewer or large needle. Add to each 25g / 1oz of crushed barley-sugar, a little noyeau, or 2 or 3 drops of essence of almonds. Fill the bottles with good unsweetened gin, cork them securely, and allow them to remain in a moderately warm place for 3 months. At the end of this time strain the liqueur through fine muslin or filtering paper until quite clear, then bottle it, cork securely, and store for use.

STRAWBERRY LIQUEUR

Half fill wide-necked glass bottles with ripe strawberries previously pricked with a fine skewer or large needle, put an equal portion of finely-crushed sugar crystals into each, and fill them with good brandy. Cork tightly, allow them to stand in a warm place for 6 weeks, then strain the liquid into small bottles, cork securely, and store for use.

VANILLA LIQUEUR

2 vanilla pods
1.7 litres / 3 pints brandy or gin
450g / 1lb granulated sugar
600ml / 1 pint water

Break the pods into short lengths, put them into the spirit, cork closely, and let it infuse for 14 days. On the last day boil the sugar and water to a thick syrup, strain the spirit into it, and when cold bottle for use.

Recipes Using Jams & Preserves

Create delicious desserts with your own home-made produce.

ALMOND AND APRICOT TARTLETS

10ml / 2 tsp apricot jam
50g / 2oz butter or margarine
50 g / 2 oz sugar
1 egg
15ml / 1 tbsp plain cake crumbs
15ml / 1 tbsp ground almonds
3 drops of almond essence
10 ml / 2 tsp nibbed almonds
15 ml / 1 tbsp Apricot Glaze (page 203)

SHORT CRUST PASTRY
100g / 4oz plain flour
1.25 ml / ¼ tsp salt
50g / 2oz margarine (or half butter, half lard) flour for rolling out

Set the oven at 190°C / 375°F / gas 5. To make the pastry, sift the flour and salt into a bowl, then rub in the margarine until the mixture resembles fine bread-crumbs. Add enough cold water to make a stiff dough. Press the dough together lightly.

Roll out the pastry on a lightly floured surface and use to line twelve 7.5 cm / 3 inch patty tins. Put a little apricot jam in each.

In a bowl, cream the butter or margarine with the sugar until pale and fluffy. Gradually beat in the egg. Stir in the cake crumbs, ground almonds and almond essence. Half fill each pastry case with the mixture and smooth the tops. Sprinkle the nibbed almonds on top.

Bake for 15 minutes or until firm to the touch. Leave the tartlets to cool. Warm the apricot glaze, brush it on top of the tartlets, then sprinkle with the chopped angelica.

MAKES TWELVE

APRICOT GLAZE

*Brush this glaze over a traditional iced cake
before applying the marzipan and icing.
Any yellow jam or marmalade may be used.*

225 g / 8 oz apricot jam

Warm the jam with 30 ml/2 tbsp water in a small saucepan over a low heat until
the jam has melted. Sieve the mixture and return the glaze to the clean pan.
Bring slowly to the boil. Allow to cool slightly before use.

**SUFFICIENT TO COAT THE TOP AND SIDES
OF 1 x 20cm / 8 inch CAKE**

BAKED JAM ROLL

butter for greasing
300g / 11oz plain flour
5ml / 1 tsp baking powder
pinch of salt
150g / 5oz shredded suet flour for rolling out
200–300g / 7–11oz jam

Grease a baking sheet. Set the oven at 190°C / 375°F / gas 5.

Sift the flour, baking powder and salt into a mixing bowl. Add the suet and enough cold water to make a soft but firm dough. On a lightly floured surface, roll the dough out to a rectangle about 5 mm / ¼ inch thick. Spread the jam almost to the edges. Dampen the edges of the pastry rectangle with water and roll up lightly. Seal the edges at either end.

Place the roll on the prepared baking sheet with the sealed edge underneath. Cover loosely with greased greaseproof paper or foil and bake for 50–60 minutes until golden brown. Transfer to a warm platter, slice and serve with warmed jam of the same type as that used in the roll.

SERVES SIX

VARIATIONS

Instead of the jam, use 200–300g / 7–11oz marmalade, or 225g / 8oz dried fruit mixed with 50g / 2oz demerara sugar. Serve with vanilla custard or a lemon sauce.

BAKED JAM SPONGE PUDDING

butter for greasing
100g / 4oz butter or margarine
100g / 4oz caster sugar
2 eggs, beaten
150g / 5oz plain flour
5ml / l tsp baking powder
1.25 ml / ¼ tsp vanilla essence
about 30ml / 2 tbsp milk
30 ml / 2 tbsp jam

Grease a 1 litre / 1¾ pint pie dish. Set the oven at 180°C / 350°F / gas 4. In a mixing bowl, cream the butter or margarine with the sugar until light and fluffy. Gradually beat in the eggs. Sift the flour and baking powder together into a bowl then fold them into the creamed mixture. Add the essence and enough milk to form a soft dropping consistency.

Put the jam in the base of the prepared pie dish. Spoon the sponge mixture on top of the jam and bake for 30–35 minutes until well risen and golden brown.

Serve from the dish with vanilla custard or jam sauce made with the same type of jam.

SERVES FOUR TO SIX

COVENTRY TURNOVERS

30ml / 2 tbsp raspberry jam
15 ml / 1 tbsp caster sugar

SHORT CRUST PASTRY
150g / 5oz plain flour
1.25ml / ¼ tsp salt
65g / 2¼oz margarine (or half butter, half lard)
flour for rolling out

Set the oven at 200°C / 400°F / gas 6. To make the pastry, sift the flour and salt into a bowl, then rub in the margarine until the mixture resembles fine bread-crumbs. Add enough cold water to make a stiff dough. Press the dough together with your fingertips.

Roll out the pastry on a lightly floured surface to a thickness of 3 mm / ⅛ inch. Cut out 8 rounds using a 10cm / 4 inch cutter. Place spoons of jam in the centre of each pastry round. Moisten the edges with water and fold the pastry over the filling. Press the edges well together and crimp or decorate with a fork.

Place the turnovers on a baking sheet, brush with water and dredge with the caster sugar. Bake for about 20 minutes or until the pastry is golden brown.

MAKES EIGHT

FREEZER TIP

When cold, open freeze on clean baking sheets, then wrap individually in freezer wrap and pack in a rigid container.

CREAM TARTLETS

30ml / 2 tbsp smooth apricot jam
250ml / 8 fl oz whipping cream
15ml / 1 tbsp icing sugar
30ml / 2 tbsp finely chopped pistachio nuts

SHORT CRUST PASTRY
100g / 4oz plain flour
1.25ml / ¼ tsp salt
50g / 2oz margarine (or half butter, half lard)
flour for rolling out

Set the oven at 200°C / 400°F / gas 6. To make the pastry, sift the flour and salt into a bowl, then rub in the margarine until the mixture resembles fine bread-crumbs. Add enough cold water to make a stiff dough. Press the dough together with your fingertips.

Roll out the pastry on a lightly floured surface and use to line twelve 7.5 cm / 3 inch patty tins. Prick the pastry, then bake the tartlets for 10 minutes. Cool completely.

When the tartlets are quite cold, put a little apricot jam in the base of each. In a bowl, whip the cream as stiffly as possible, gradually adding the sugar. Put the cream into a piping bag fitted with a 1cm / ½ inch nozzle and pipe in swirls and peaks over the jam. Sprinkle with the chopped pistachios.

MAKES TWELVE

DEAN'S CREAM

This is a very old recipe for a dessert that was one of the
forerunners of the standard modern trifle.

6 individual sponge cakes
raspberry jam
apricot jam
100g / 4oz ratafias
250ml / 8 fl oz sherry
75ml / 5 tbsp brandy
500 ml / 17 fl oz double cream
50g / 2oz caster sugar

DECORATION
angelica
glacé cherries
crystallized pineapple

Cut the sponge cakes in half lengthways, and spread half with raspberry jam and half with apricot jam. Arrange them in a deep glass dish, jam sides upwards.

Break the ratafias into pieces and sprinkle on top of the sponge cakes. Pour the sherry over the cakes and leave to soak for about 30 minutes.

Put the brandy, cream, and sugar into a bowl and whisk until very thick. Pile into the dish and decorate with angelica, cherries, and crystallized pineapple. Chill well before serving.

SERVES EIGHT

EMPRESS PUDDING

butter for greasing
100g / 4oz long-grain rice
1 litre / 1¾ pints milk
pinch of salt
50g / 2oz butter or margarine
50g / 2oz caster sugar
200g / 7oz jam or stewed fruit

SHORT CRUST PASTRY
75g / 3oz plain flour
pinch of salt
40g / 1½oz margarine (or half butter, half lard)
flour for rolling out

Butter the base of a 1.25 litre / 2¼ pint ovenproof dish. Make the pastry. Sift the flour and salt into a bowl, then rub in the margarine until the mixture resembles fine breadcrumbs. Add enough cold water to make a stiff dough. Press the dough together with your fingertips. Set the pastry aside in a cool place while preparing the rice filling.

Wash the rice, drain and place in a heavy bottomed saucepan. Add the milk and salt and simmer for about 1 hour or until tender. Stir in the butter or margarine and sugar.

Set the oven at 180°C / 350°F / gas 4. Roll out the pastry on a lightly floured surface and line the sides of the baking dish. Spread a layer of the rice mixture on the base of the dish and cover with jam or fruit. Repeat the layers until the dish is full, finishing with a layer of rice. Bake for 25–30 minutes.

SERVES SIX

EVERYDAY PANCAKES

Pancakes are much too good to be reserved exclusively for Shrove Tuesday. Simple, versatile, and always popular, they lend themselves to a wide range of preserved fillings.

100g / 4oz plain flour
1.25 ml / ¼ tsp salt
1 egg, beaten
250 ml / 8 fl oz milk, or half milk and half water
oil for frying

Make the batter. Sift the flour and salt into a bowl, make a well in the centre and add the beaten egg. Stir in half the milk (or all the milk, if using a mixture of milk and water), gradually working the flour down from the sides. Beat vigorously until the mixture is smooth and bubbly, then stir in the rest of the milk (or the water). Pour into a jug. The mixture may be left to stand at this stage, in which case it should be covered and stored in the refrigerator.

Heat a little oil in a clean 18cm / 7 inch pancake pan. Pour off any excess oil, leaving the pan covered with a thin film of grease. Stir the batter and pour about 30–45 ml / 2–3 tbsp into the pan. There should be just enough to thinly cover the base. Tilt and rotate the pan so that the batter runs over the surface evenly.

Cook over moderate heat for about 1 minute until the pancake is set and golden brown underneath. Make sure the pancake is loose by shaking the pan, then either toss it or turn it with a palette knife or fish slice. Cook the second side for about 30 seconds or until golden. Slide the pancake out on to a warmed plate. Serve at once, with a suitable filling or sauce, or keep warm over simmering water or in a very low oven while making more pancakes in the same way. Add more oil to the pan when necessary.

MAKES EIGHT

SERVING SUGGESTION

Spoon ice cream into the centre of each pancake and fold in half like an omelette. Serve at once with Jam Sauce (page 215).

FOREST PUDDING

butter or oil for greasing
3 pieces of plain cake or trifle sponges
jam
5ml / 1 tsp grated lemon rind
500ml / 17 fl oz milk
2 eggs
25g / 1oz caster sugar

Grease a 750ml / 1¼ pint pie dish. Cut the cake vertically into 1cm / ¼ inch slices and sandwich in pairs with the jam. Place the cake sandwiches in the pie dish and sprinkle with the lemon rind. Set aside.

In a saucepan, warm the milk to about 65°C / 150°F; do not let it approach boiling point.

Put the eggs and sugar into a bowl, mix well, then stir in the warm milk. Strain the custard mixture into the dish and leave to stand for 1 hour. Meanwhile set the oven at 140–150°C / 275–300°F / gas 1–2.

Bake the pudding for 1–1½ hours until the custard is set and the pudding browned on top. Serve hot.

SERVES FOUR

FROSTED APPLES

oil for greasing
6 cooking apples (about 800g / 1¾lb)
30ml / 2 tbsp lemon juice
100g / 4oz granulated sugar
15ml / 1 tbsp fine-cut orange marmalade
2.5cm / 1 inch cinnamon stick
2 cloves
2 egg whites
100g / 4oz caster sugar, plus extra
for dusting

DECORATION
125ml / 4 fl oz double cream
glacé cherries
angelica

Line a large baking sheet with greaseproof paper or non-stick baking parchment. Oil the lining paper. Set the oven at 180°C / 350°F / gas 4.

Wash, core and peel the apples, leaving them whole. Reserve the peelings. Brush the apples all over with the lemon juice to preserve the colour.

Combine the granulated sugar, marmalade, cinnamon stick, cloves and apple peelings in a large saucepan. Stir in 250ml / 8 fl oz water. Heat gently, stirring occasionally, until the sugar and marmalade have melted, then boil for 2–3 minutes without stirring to make a thin syrup.

Place the apples in a baking dish and strain the syrup over them. Cover with a lid or foil and bake for about 30 minutes or until the apples are just tender. Lower the oven temperature to 120°C / 250°F / gas ½.

Using a slotted spoon, carefully remove the apples from the syrup, dry well on absorbent kitchen paper, then place on the prepared baking sheet.

Whisk the egg whites in a clean, grease-free bowl until they form stiff peaks, then gradually whisk in the caster sugar, a teaspoon at a time (see Mrs Beeton's Tip).

Coat each apple completely with the meringue, and dust lightly with caster sugar. Return to the oven and bake for about 1½ hours or until the meringue is firm and very lightly coloured. Remove from the oven and leave to cool.

In a bowl, whip the cream until it just holds its shape. Pile a spoonful on top of each apple and decorate with small pieces of cherry and angelica. Serve the apples on a bed of whipped cream in individual bowls, or with the cold baking syrup poured over them.

SERVES SIX

MRS BEETON'S TIP

If using an electric whisk to make the meringue, whisk in all the sugar. If whisking by hand, however, whisk in only half the sugar and fold in the rest.

JAM MUFFINS

Unlike English muffins, American muffins are quick breads.
They are light, savoury or sweet buns made with slightly more puffed,
richer dough than scones. They are very popular breakfast breads.

butter for greasing
200g / 7oz plain flour
15ml / 1 tbsp baking powder
2.5 ml / ½ tsp salt
50g / 2oz granulated sugar
50g / 2oz butter
1 egg
200ml / 7 fl oz milk
60ml / 4 tbsp jam

Butter twelve 6cm / 2¼ inch muffin tins or deep bun tins. Set the oven at 200°C / 400°F / gas 6. Sift the dry ingredients into a bowl.

Melt the butter. Mix with the egg and milk in a separate bowl. Pour the liquid mixture over the dry ingredients. Stir only enough to dampen the flour; the mixture should be lumpy. Spoon into the prepared muffin tins, as lightly as possible, filling them only two thirds full. Top each muffin with 5ml / 1 tsp jam.

Bake for about 15 minutes, until well risen and browned. The cooked muffins should be cracked across the middle. Cool in the tins for 2–3 minutes, then turn out on to a wire rack to finish cooling.

MAKES TWELVE

JAM SAUCE

Simple sauces can be highly successful.
Try Jam Sauce on steamed or baked puddings.

60ml / 4 tbsp seedless jam
lemon juice
10ml / 2 tsp arrowroot
few drops of food colouring (optional)

Put the jam in a saucepan with 250ml / 8 fl oz water and bring to the boil. Add lemon juice to taste. In a cup, mix the arrowroot with a little cold water until smooth. Stir into the hot liquid and heat gently until the sauce thickens, stirring constantly. Add a little colouring if necessary. Pour into a jug and serve at once.

MAKES ABOUT 300ml / ½ pint

JAM TART

60–90ml / 4–6 tbsp firm jam
beaten egg for glazing

SHORT CRUST PASTRY
150g / 5oz plain flour
2.5ml / ½ tsp salt
65g / 2¼ oz margarine (or half butter, half lard)
flour for rolling out

Set the oven at 200°C / 400°F / gas 6. To make the pastry, sift the flour and salt into a bowl then rub in the margarine until the mixture resembles fine breadcrumbs. Add enough cold water to make a stiff dough. Press the dough together lightly. Roll out the pastry on a lightly floured surface and use to line a 20 cm / 8 inch pie plate. Decorate the edge with any trimmings. Fill with jam and glaze the uncovered pastry with beaten egg. Bake for 15 minutes or until the pastry is cooked. Serve hot or cold.

SERVES SIX

JAPANESE PLOMBIERE

*A plombière is an ice cream mixture containing almonds or chestnuts.
It may be frozen in a decorative mould but is more often scooped
into balls and piled up to form a pyramid. It is often served with
a sauce poured over the top.*

50g / 2oz apricot jam
few drops of lemon juice
8 egg yolks
100g / 4oz caster sugar
500ml / 17 fl oz single cream
2.5ml / ½ tsp vanilla essence
100g / 4oz ground almonds
250ml / 8 fl oz double cream
100g / 4oz almond macaroons, crushed
12 ratafias to decorate

Turn the freezing compartment or freezer to the coldest setting about 1 hour
before making the ice cream.

Make an apricot marmalade by boiling the apricot jam in a small saucepan with
a few drops of lemon juice until thick. Keep a little aside for decoration and
sieve the rest into a bowl.

MICROWAVE TIP

*The apricot marmalade may be
prepared in a small bowl in the
microwave. It will only require about
30 seconds on High. Reheat it, if
necessary, before pouring it over the
ice cream pyramid.*

Combine the egg yolks and caster sugar in a deep bowl and beat together until very thick. Put the single cream in a saucepan and bring slowly to the boil. Pour the cream over the yolks and sugar, stirring well. Return the mixture to the clean pan. Cook, stirring constantly, until the custard thickens. Do not allow it to boil. Pour the thickened custard into a large bowl and stir in the sieved apricot marmalade, the vanilla essence and the ground almonds. Cover closely with dampened greaseproof paper and cool.

In a bowl, whip the double cream to the same consistency as the custard. Fold it into the custard, with the crushed macaroons. Spoon the mixture into a suitable container for freezing (a bowl that is deep enough to allow the ice cream to be scooped is ideal). Freeze the mixture until firm.

To serve, scoop into balls, arranging these as a pyramid on a chilled plate. Drizzle the reserved apricot marmalade over the top and decorate with the ratafias.

SERVES SIX TO EIGHT

JIM-JAMS

butter for greasing
150g / 5oz plain flour
50g / 2oz ground almonds
1.25ml / ¼ tsp salt
100g / 4oz butter or margarine
100g / 4oz caster sugar
1 egg yolk
flour for rolling
strawberry jam for filling
sifted icing sugar for dredging

Thoroughly grease two or three baking sheets. Set the oven at 180°C / 350°F / gas 4. Mix the flour, ground almonds and salt in a bowl.

In a mixing bowl, beat the butter or margarine until soft, add the sugar and continue to beat until light and fluffy. Beat in the egg yolk. Fold in the flour mixture, first using a knife and then the fingers.

Knead the biscuit dough lightly on a floured surface, then roll out to a thickness of 5 mm / ¼ inch. Cut the dough into rounds with a 6cm / 2¼ inch cutter. Re-roll and re-cut trimmings.

Place the biscuits on the prepared baking sheets, pricking the top of each in several places. Bake for 12–15 minutes, until golden. Leave to stand for 5 minutes, then cool on a wire rack.

When quite cold, sandwich the biscuits together in pairs with strawberry jam and dredge with icing sugar, if liked.

MAKES TWENTY-FIVE TO THIRTY

MARMALADE AND WINE SAUCE

Baked puddings can be somewhat dry.
This zesty sauce is the perfect accompaniment.

90ml / 6 tbsp orange marmalade
90ml / 6 tbsp white wine

Combine the marmalade and wine in a saucepan and heat gently for 5 minutes.
Transfer to a jug and serve at once.

MAKES ABOUT 175ml / 6 fl oz

MILLE-FEUILLE GATEAU

PUFF PASTRY
200g / 7oz plain flour
1.25ml / ¼ tsp salt
200g / 7oz butter
2.5ml / ½ tsp lemon juice
flour for rolling out

FILLING AND TOPPING
300ml / ½ pint double cream
100g / 4oz icing sugar, sifted
100g / 4oz raspberry jam

Make the pastry. Sift the flour and salt into a mixing bowl and rub in 50g /2oz of the butter. Add the lemon juice and mix to a smooth dough with cold water. Shape the remaining butter into a rectangle on greaseproof paper. Roll out the dough on a lightly floured surface to a strip a little wider than the butter and rather more than twice its length. Place the butter on one half of the pastry, fold the other half over it, and press the edges together with the rolling pin. Leave in a cool place for 15 minutes to allow the butter to harden.

Roll the pastry out into a long strip. Fold the bottom third up and the top third down, press the edges together with the rolling pin and turn the pastry so that the folded edges are on the right and left. Roll and fold again, cover and leave in a cool place for 15 minutes. Repeat this process until the pastry has been rolled out 6 times (see Mrs Beeton's Tip). Chill the pastry well between each rolling, wrapping it in cling film to prevent it drying on the surface. The pastry is now ready for use.

Set the oven at 230°C / 450°F / gas 8. Roll out the pastry on a lightly floured surface to a thickness of 3mm / ⅛ inch. Cut into six 15cm / 6 inch rounds. If work surface space is limited, it is best to cut the pastry into portions to do this. Either cut the pastry into six portions or cut it in half and cut out three circles from each half.

Place the pastry circles on baking sheets, prick well and bake for 8–10 minutes until crisp and golden brown. Lift the rounds off carefully and cool on wire racks.

In a bowl, whip the cream until thick. Make glacé icing by mixing the icing sugar with enough cold water to form an icing that will coat the back of the spoon. Coat one pastry layer with icing and set aside for the lid. Sandwich the remaining layers together lightly with the jam and cream. Put the iced layer on top. Sieve as soon as possible.

SERVES SIX TO EIGHT

MRS BEETON'S TIP

*Never rush the process of making puff pastry:
always chill it if the fat begins to melt. It is a good
idea to mark the pastry each time it is rolled,
as it is easy to lose track of the number of times
this process has been carried out.*

MRS BEETON'S BAKEWELL PUDDING

strawberry or apricot jam
50g / 2oz butter
50g / 2oz caster sugar
1 egg
50g / 2oz ground almonds
50g / 2oz fine cake crumbs
few drops of almond essence
icing sugar for dusting

SHORT CRUST PASTRY
100g / 4oz plain flour
1.25ml / ¼ tsp salt
50g / 2oz margarine (or half butter, half lard)
flour for rolling out

Set the oven at 200°C / 400°F / gas 6. To make the pastry, sift the flour and salt into a bowl, then rub in the margarine until the mixture resembles fine bread-crumbs. Add enough cold water to make a stiff dough. Press the dough together. Roll out the pastry on a lightly floured surface and use to line an 18cm / 7 inch flan tin or ring placed on a baking sheet. Spread a good layer of jam over the pastry base.

In a mixing bowl, cream the butter with the sugar until pale and fluffy. Beat in the egg, and then add the almonds, cake crumbs and essence. Beat until well mixed. Pour into the flan case, on top of the jam.

Bake for 30 minutes or until the centre of the pudding is firm. Sprinkle with icing sugar and serve hot or cold.

SERVES FOUR TO FIVE

MRS BEETON'S CUSTARD TARTLETS

1 sheet ready-rolled puff pastry, about 250–300g / 9–11oz
flour for rolling out
25g / 1oz butter
scant 75ml / 5 tbsp icing sugar
15ml / 1 tbsp plain flour
3 eggs
250ml / 8 fl oz milk
few drops of vanilla essence
30ml / 2 tbsp whole fruit strawberry or blackcurrant jam,
plus extra to decorate

Roll out the pastry on a lightly floured surface to 5mm / ¼ inch thick. Leave to rest while preparing the custard.

Cream the butter and sugar in a bowl, then mix in the flour until well blended. Whisk the eggs into the milk and add the vanilla essence. Blend the mixture gradually into the butter and sugar, breaking down any lumps. Heat gently in a heavy saucepan, stirring all the time, until the mixture reaches simmering point and thickens. Remove from the heat, cover with damp greaseproof paper and leave to cool while preparing the pastry cases. Set the oven at 190°C / 375°F / gas 5.

Line twelve 7.5cm / 3 inch patty tins, about 1cm / ½ inch deep, with the pastry, pressing it in well. Put a little of the jam in the bottom of each pastry case. Spoon the custard mixture over the jam, almost filling the cases.

Bake for 20–25 minutes, until the custard is firm. Cool in the tins. Before serving, decorate each tartlet with a small dab of additional jam in the centre.

MAKES TWELVE

MRS BEETON'S MANCHESTER PUDDING

250ml / 8 fl oz milk
2 strips of lemon rind
75g / 3oz fresh white breadcrumbs
2 whole eggs plus 2 egg yolks
50g / 2oz butter, softened
45ml / 3 tbsp caster sugar
45ml / 3 tbsp brandy
45–60ml / 3–4 tbsp jam
extra caster sugar for sprinkling

PUFF PASTRY
50g / 5 oz plain flour
1.25ml / ¼ tsp salt
150g / 5oz butter
2.5ml / ½ tsp lemon juice
flour for rolling out

Heat the milk in a saucepan with the lemon rind, then remove from the heat and leave to infuse for 30 minutes. Put the breadcrumbs in a bowl, strain the flavoured milk over them and return the mixture to the clean pan. Simmer for 2–3 minutes or until the crumbs have absorbed all the milk.

Beat the eggs and yolks until liquid, then stir into the breadcrumbs with the butter, sugar and brandy. Mix thoroughly; the butter should melt in the warm mixture. Cover the surface with dampened greaseproof paper and leave to cool. Set the oven at 200°C / 400°F / gas 6. Make the pastry. Sift the flour and salt into a mixing bowl and rub in 50g / 2oz of the butter. Add the lemon juice and mix to a smooth dough with cold water.

Shape the remaining butter into a rectangle on greaseproof paper. Roll out the dough on a lightly floured surface to a strip a little wider than the butter and rather more than twice its length. Place the butter on one half of the pastry, fold the other half over it, and press the edges together with the rolling pin. Leave in a cool place for 15 minutes to allow the butter to harden.

Roll out the pastry into a long strip. Fold the bottom third up and the top third down, press the edges together with the rolling pin and turn the pastry so that the folded edges are on the right and left. Roll and fold again, cover and leave in a cool place for 15 minutes. Repeat this process until the pastry has been rolled out 6 times.

Line a 750ml / 1¼ pint pie dish with the pastry. If liked, cut a strip out of the pastry trimmings to fit the rim of the pie dish. Dampen the rim of the lining and fit the extra strip. Wrap any remaining pastry and reserve in the refrigerator for another purpose.

Spread the jam over the base of the pastry. Spoon the cooled breadcrumb mixture into the pastry case and bake for 15 minutes, then lower the heat to 180°C / 350°F / gas 4 and cook for 45–60 minutes more. The pudding should be set in the centre. Leave to cool. Serve cold, sprinkled with caster sugar.

SERVES SIX

MRS BEETON'S TRIFLE

Plain whisked or creamed sponge cake, individual buns,
or Madeira cake are ideal for this trifle. Originally, Mrs Beeton made
her custard by using 8 eggs to thicken 600ml / 1 pint milk, cooking
it slowly over hot water. Using cornflour and egg yolks is more
practical and it gives a creamier, less 'eggy' result.

4 slices of plain cake or individual cakes
6 almond macaroons
12 ratafias
175ml / 6 fl oz sherry
30–45ml / 2–3 tbsp brandy
60–90ml / 4–6 tbsp raspberry or strawberry jam
grated rind of ½ lemon
25g / 1oz flaked almonds
300ml / ½ pint double cream
30ml / 2 tbsp icing sugar
candied and crystallized fruit and peel to decorate

CUSTARD
25g / 1oz cornflour
25g / 1oz caster sugar
4 egg yolks
5ml / 1 tsp vanilla essence
600ml / 1 pint milk

Place the sponge cakes in a glass dish. Add the macaroons and ratafias, pressing them down gently. Pour about 50ml / 2 fl oz of the sherry into a basin and set it aside, then pour the rest over the biscuits and cake. Sprinkle with the brandy. Warm the jam in a small saucepan, then pour it evenly over the trifle base, spreading it lightly. Top with the lemon rind and almonds.

For the custard, blend the cornflour, caster sugar, egg yolks and vanilla to a smooth cream with a little of the milk. Heat the remaining milk until hot. Pour some of the milk on the egg mixture, stirring, then replace the mixture in the saucepan with the rest of the milk. Bring to the boil, stirring constantly, and simmer for 3 minutes. Pour the custard over the trifle base and cover the surface with a piece of dampened greaseproof paper. Set aside to cool.

Add the cream and icing sugar to the reserved sherry and whip until the mixture stands in soft peaks. Swirl the cream over the top of the trifle and chill. Decorate with pieces of candied and crystallized fruit and peel before serving.

SERVES SIX

PADDINGTON PUDDING

butter for greasing
100g / 4oz dried white breadcrumbs
100g / 4oz sultanas
100g / 4oz shredded suet
100g / 4oz self-raising flour
grated rind of 1 lemon
50g / 2oz caster sugar
pinch of salt
60ml / 4 tbsp marmalade
2 eggs, beaten
about 75ml / 3 fl oz milk

Grease a 1-litre / 1¾-pint pudding basin. Prepare a steamer or half fill a large saucepan with water and bring to the boil. Mix the breadcrumbs, sultanas, suet, flour, grated rind, sugar, salt and marmalade in a mixing bowl. Stir in the beaten eggs with enough milk to give a dropping consistency. Spoon the mixture into the prepared basin, cover with greased greaseproof paper and foil and secure with string.

Put the pudding in the perforated part of the steamer, or stand it on an old saucer or plate in the pan of boiling water. The water should come halfway up the sides of the basin. Cover the pan tightly and steam the pudding over gently simmering water for 1½–2 hours. Leave for 5–10 minutes at room temperature to firm up, then turn out on to a serving plate. Serve with single cream or custard.

SERVES SIX

PATRIOTIC PUDDING

butter for greasing
45ml / 3 tbsp red jam
200g / 7oz plain flour
pinch of salt
10ml / 2 tsp baking powder
100g / 4oz butter or margarine
100g / 4oz caster sugar
1 egg, beaten
about 75ml / 3 fl oz milk

Grease a 1 litre / 1¾ pint pudding basin and cover the base with the jam. Prepare a steamer or half fill a large saucepan with water and bring to the boil.

Sift the flour, salt and baking powder into a mixing bowl. Rub in the butter or margarine and add the sugar. Stir in the egg and milk to give a soft dropping consistency. Spoon the mixture into the prepared basin, cover with greased greaseproof paper and foil and secure with string.

Put the pudding in the perforated part of the steamer, or stand it on an old saucer or plate in the pan of boiling water. The water should come halfway up the sides of the basin. Cover the pan tightly and steam the pudding over gently simmering water for 1½–2 hours.

SERVES SIX

PEARS IN WINE

100g / 4oz sugar
30ml / 2 tbsp redcurrant jelly
1.5cm / ¾ inch cinnamon stick
4 large ripe cooking pears (about 450g / 1lb)
250ml / 8 fl oz red wine
25g / 1oz flaked almonds

Combine the sugar, redcurrant jelly and cinnamon stick in a saucepan wide enough to hold all the pears upright so that they fit snugly and will not fall over. Add 250ml / 8 fl oz water and heat gently, stirring constantly, until the sugar and jelly have dissolved.

Peel the pears, leaving the stalks in place. Carefully remove as much of the core as possible without breaking the fruit. Stand the pears upright in the pan, cover, and simmer gently for 15 minutes.

Add the wine and cook, uncovered, for 15 minutes more. Remove the pears carefully with a slotted spoon, arrange them on a serving dish.

Remove the cinnamon stick from the pan and add the almonds. Boil the liquid remaining in the pan rapidly until it is reduced to a thin syrup. Pour the syrup over the pears and serve warm. This dessert can also be served cold. Pour the hot syrup over the pears, leave to cool, then chill before serving.

SERVES FOUR

PLAIN SCONES

butter for greasing
225g / 8oz self-raising flour
2.5ml / ½ tsp salt
25–50g / 1–2oz butter or margarine
125–150ml / 4–5 fl oz milk
flour for kneading
milk or beaten egg for glazing (optional)

Grease a baking sheet. Set the oven at 220°C / 425°F / gas 7. Sift the flour and salt into a large bowl. Rub in the butter or margarine, then mix to a soft dough with the milk, using a round-bladed knife. Knead very lightly on a floured surface until smooth.

Roll or pat out the dough to about 1cm / ½ inch thick and cut into rounds, using a 6cm / 2½ inch cutter. (Alternatively, divide into two equal portions and roll each piece into a round 1–2cm / ½–¾ inch thick. Mark each round into six wedges.) Re-roll the trimmings and re-cut.

Place the scones on the prepared baking sheet. Brush the tops with milk or beaten egg, if liked. Bake for 10–12 minutes. Cool on a wire rack. Serve with butter, jam, clotted cream and tea from a teapot.

MAKES TWELVE

OTHER RAISING AGENTS

Scones can be made using plain flour with raising agents: for 225g / 8oz plain flour, use 5ml / 1 tsp bicarbonate of soda and 10ml / 2 tsp cream of tartar. Or use 20ml / 4 tsp baking powder as the raising agent.

PORT WINE JELLY

25ml / 5 tsp gelatine
50g / 2oz sugar
30ml / 2 tbsp redcurrant jelly
250ml / 8 fl oz port
few drops of red food colouring

Place 30ml / 2 tbsp water in a small bowl and sprinkle the gelatine on to the liquid. Set aside for 15 minutes until the gelatine is spongy. Stand the bowl over a saucepan of hot water and stir the gelatine until it has dissolved.

Combine the sugar and redcurrant jelly in a pan. Add 400ml / 14 fl oz water and heat gently, stirring constantly, until all the sugar has dissolved.

Add the gelatine liquid to the syrup and stir in the port and food colouring. Pour through a strainer lined with a single thickness of scalded fine cotton or muslin into a wetted 900-ml / 1½-pint mould. Chill until set.

SERVES SIX

QUEEN OF PUDDINGS

butter for greasing
75g / 3oz fresh white breadcrumbs
400ml / 14 fl oz milk
25g / 1oz butter
10ml / 2 tsp grated lemon rind
2 eggs, separated
75g / 3oz caster sugar
30ml / 2 tbsp red jam

Grease a 750ml / 1¼ pint pie dish. Set the oven at 160°C / 325°F / gas 3. Spread the breadcrumbs out on a baking sheet and put into the oven to dry off slightly.

Warm the milk and butter with the lemon rind in a saucepan. Meanwhile put the egg yolks in a bowl and stir in 25g / 1oz of the sugar. Pour on the warmed milk mixture, stirring thoroughly. Add the breadcrumbs, mix thoroughly and pour into the prepared pie dish. Leave to stand for 30 minutes.

Bake the pudding for 40–50 minutes until lightly set, then remove from the oven. Lower the oven temperature to 120°C / 250°F / gas 1. Warm the jam in a small saucepan until runny, then spread it over the top of the pudding.

In a clean, grease-free bowl, whisk the egg whites until stiff. Add half the remaining sugar and whisk again. Fold in all but 15ml / 1 tbsp of the remaining sugar. Spoon the meringue around the edge of the jam, drawing it up into peaks at regular intervals to resemble a crown. Sprinkle with the rest of the sugar.

Return the pudding to the oven and bake for 40–45 minutes more, until the meringue is set.

SERVES FOUR

RASPBERRY BUNS

butter for greasing
200g / 7oz self-raising flour
1.25ml / ¼ tsp salt
75g / 3oz margarine
75g / 3oz sugar
1 egg
milk (see method)
60–75ml / 4–5 tbsp raspberry jam
beaten egg for brushing
caster sugar for sprinkling

Grease two baking sheets. Set the oven at 200°C / 400°F / gas 6. Sift the flour and salt into a mixing bowl. Rub in the margarine until the mixture resembles fine breadcrumbs. Stir in the sugar. Put the egg into a measuring jug and add enough milk to make up to 125ml / 4 fl oz. Add the liquid to the dry ingredients and mix with a fork to a sticky stiff mixture that will support the fork. Divide the mixture into 12–14 portions. Form into 12–14 balls with lightly floured hands. Make a deep dent in the centre of each and drop 5ml / 1 tsp raspberry jam inside. Close the bun mixture over the jam. Brush with egg and sprinkle with sugar, then arrange on the prepared sheets, allowing about 2 cm/ ¾ inch between each for spreading. Bake for 15–20 minutes or until each bun is firm to the touch on the base. Cool on a wire rack.

MAKES TWELVE TO FOURTEEN

REDCURRANT SAUCE

100g / 4oz redcurrant jelly
45ml / 3 tbsp port

Combine the jelly and port in a small pan and cook over gentle heat until the jelly melts. Pour over steamed puddings or serve with hot milk puddings such as semolina. The sauce also makes a good glaze for berry-topped cheesecakes.

MAKES ABOUT 150ml / ¼ pint

RING O' ROSES

butter for greasing
100g / 4oz margarine
50g / 2oz caster sugar
1 egg yolk
100g / 4oz plain flour
flour for rolling out

ALMOND TOPPING
1 egg white
75g / 3oz caster sugar
50g / 2oz ground almonds

DECORATION
60ml / 4 tbsp red jam or jelly

Grease a baking sheet. Set the oven at 180°C / 350°F / gas 4. In a mixing bowl, cream the margarine and sugar thoroughly. Work in the egg yolk and then the flour to form a dough. On a lightly floured surface, knead well, then roll out to a thickness of 5mm / ¼ inch. Cut into 4cm / 1½ inch rounds. Place on the prepared baking sheet.

Make the almond topping. In a bowl, whisk the egg white until frothy, then stir in the caster sugar and the ground almonds. Using a piping bag fitted with a plain nozzle, pipe a circle of the almond mixture around the edge of each biscuit. Bake for 15 minutes, then cool on the baking sheet. When cold, fill the centres of the biscuits with jam or jelly.

MAKES TWELVE

SOUFFLE OMELETTE

*Soufflé omelettes are quick and easy to make – the perfect finale for
the busy cook. Fill simply with 45ml / 3 tbsp warmed jam.*

**2 eggs, separated
5ml / 1 tsp caster sugar
few drops of vanilla essence
15ml / 1 tbsp unsalted butter or margarine
icing sugar for dredging**

In a large bowl, whisk the yolks until creamy. Add the sugar and vanilla essence
with 30ml / 2 tbsp water, then whisk again. In a clean, grease-free bowl, whisk
the egg whites until stiff and matt.

Place an 18cm / 7 inch omelette pan over gentle heat and when it is hot, add the
butter or margarine. Tilt the pan to grease the whole of the inside. Pour out any
excess. Fold the egg whites into the yolk mixture carefully until evenly distrib-
uted, using a metal spoon (see Mrs Beeton's Tip). Heat the grill to moderate.

Pour the egg mixture into the omelette pan, level the top very lightly, and cook
for 1–2 minutes over moderate heat until the omelette is golden brown on the
underside and moist on top. (Use a palette knife to lift the edge of the omelette
to look underneath.)

Put the pan under the grill for 5–6 minutes until the omelette is risen and lightly
browned on the top. The texture of the omelette should be firm yet spongy.

MRS BEETON'S TIP

*When folding the beaten egg whites
into the omelette mixture, be very
careful not to overmix, as it is the air
incorporated in the frothy whites that
causes the omelette to rise.*

Remove from the heat as soon as it is ready, as over-cooking tends to make it tough. Run a palette knife gently round the edge and underneath to loosen it. Make a mark across the middle at right angles to the pan handle but do not cut the surface. Put the chosen filling on one half, raise the handle of the pan and double the omelette over. Turn gently on to a warm plate, dredge with icing sugar and serve at once.

SERVES ONE

FILLINGS

- **Cherry Omelette** Stone 100g / 4oz dark cherries, or use canned ones. Warm with 30ml / 2 tbsp cherry jam and 15ml / 1 tbsp kirsch. Spread over the omelette.
- **Jam Omelette** Warm 45ml / 3 tbsp fruity jam and spread over the omelette.
- **Lemon Omelette** Add the grated rind of ½ lemon to the egg yolks. Warm 45ml / 3 tbsp lemon curd with 10ml / 2 tsp lemon juice, and spread over the omelette.
- **Orange Chocolate Omelette** Warm 15ml / 1 tbsp orange marmalade and mix with 30ml / 2 tbsp chocolate spread. Spread over the omelette.

SPECIAL EFFECTS

- **Flambé Omelette** Warm 30ml / 2 tbsp rum or brandy. Put the cooked omelette on to a warm plate, pour the warmed spirit round it, ignite, and serve immediately.
- **Branded Omelettes** Soufflé omelettes are sometimes 'branded' for a special occasion. A lattice decoration is marked on the top using hot skewers. Heat the pointed ends of three metal skewers until red-hot. When the omelette is on the plate, dredge with icing sugar. Protecting your hand in an oven glove, quickly press the hot skewers, one at a time, on to the sugar, holding them there until the sugar caramelizes. Make a diagonal criss-cross design. Each skewer should make two marks if you work quickly.

SWEET SHERRY SAUCE

75ml / 5 tbsp sherry
30ml / 2 tbsp seedless jam or jelly
lemon juice

Combine the sherry and jam in a saucepan. Add 75ml / 5 tbsp water with lemon juice to taste. Bring to the boil and boil for 2–3 minutes. Strain, if necessary, before serving in a jug or sauceboat.

MAKES ABOUT 150ml / ¼ pint

SWISS ROLL

butter for greasing
3 eggs
75g / 3oz caster sugar
75g / 3oz plain flour
2.5ml / ½ tsp baking powder
pinch of salt
about 60ml / 4 tbsp jam for filling
caster sugar for dusting

Line and grease a 30 x 20 cm / 12 x 8 inch Swiss roll tin. Set the oven at 220°C / 425°F / gas 7. Combine the eggs and sugar in a heatproof bowl. Set the bowl over a pan of hot water, taking care that the bottom of the bowl does not touch the water. Whisk for 10–15 minutes until thick and creamy, then remove from the pan. Continue whisking until the mixture is cold. Sift the flour, baking powder and salt into a bowl, then lightly fold into the egg mixture. Pour into the prepared tin and bake for 10 minutes. Meanwhile warm the jam in a small saucepan.

When the cake is cooked, turn it on to a large sheet of greaseproof paper dusted with caster sugar. Peel off the lining paper. Trim off any crisp edges. Spread the cake with the warmed jam and roll up tightly from one long side. Dredge with caster sugar and place on a wire rack, with the join underneath to cool.

MAKES ONE 30cm / 12 inch SWISS ROLL

VICTORIA SANDWICH CAKE

The original Victoria Sandwich was oblong, filled with jam or marmalade and cut into fingers or sandwiches. Now, the basic mixture is used with many different flavourings and fillings and is served as a single, round cake. For a softer-centred cake bake the mixture in a 20cm / 8 inch round cake tin, then split and fill. All loose crumbs must be brushed off before filling. Keep the filling fairly firm – if it is too moist, it will seep into the cake.

butter for greasing
150g / 5oz butter or margarine
150g / 5oz caster sugar
3 eggs, beaten
150g / 5oz self-raising flour or plain flour and
5ml / 1 tsp baking powder
pinch of salt
raspberry or other jam for filling
caster sugar for dredging

Line and grease two 18cm / 7 inch sandwich tins. Set the oven at 180°C / 350°F / gas 4.

In a mixing bowl cream the butter or margarine with the sugar until light and fluffy. Add the eggs gradually, beating well after each addition. Sift the flour, salt and baking powder, if used, into a bowl. Stir into the creamed mixture, lightly but thoroughly, until evenly mixed.

Divide between the tins and bake for 25–30 minutes. Cool on a wire rack, then sandwich together with jam. Sprinkle the top with caster or icing sugar.

MAKES ONE 18cm / 7 inch CAKE

VICTORIA SANDWICH, ONE-STAGE

butter for greasing
150g / 5oz self-raising flour
pinch of salt
150g / 5oz soft margarine
150g / 5oz caster sugar
3 eggs

Line and grease two 18 cm / 7 inch sandwich tins. Set the oven at 180°C / 350°F / gas 4. Put all the ingredients in a mixing bowl and stir. Beat until smooth, allowing 2–3 minutes by hand or 1–1½ minutes with an electric mixer. Divide the mixture evenly between the tins; level each surface. Bake for 25–30 minutes. Cool on a wire rack, then fill and top as desired.

MAKES ONE 18cm / 7 inch CAKE

FILLINGS FOR VICTORIA SANDWICH CAKES

- **Harlequin Sandwich Cake** Make the cake mixture as in the main recipe, then put half in one sandwich tin. Add pink food colouring to the second portion of mixture, making it a fairly strong colour. Put the second portion in the other sandwich tin and bake the cake. When cool, cut both cakes into rings: cut a 5cm / 2 inch circle from the middle of each cake, then cut a 10cm / 4 inch circle around it. Either use plain pastry cutters or cut out circles of paper and use a pointed knife to cut around them. You should have three rings of each cake. Carefully put the rings of cake together alternating the colours to make two layers. Sandwich the layers together with raspberry jam. Spread warmed raspberry jam over the top of the cake and sift icing sugar over it.
- **Lemon Sandwich Cake** Add the grated rind of 1 large lemon to the fat and sugar. Continue as in the main recipe, then sandwich the cooled cakes together with lemon curd.
- **Orange Sandwich Cake** Add the grated rind of 1 large orange to the fat and sugar, then continue as in the main recipe. Sandwich the cooled cakes together with orange marmalade.

WASHINGTON RIPPLE

butter for greasing
150g / 5oz butter or margarine
150g / 5oz caster sugar
3 eggs, beaten
150g / 5oz plain flour
5ml / 1 tsp baking powder
30ml / 2 tbsp raspberry jam or jelly

Grease a 1 litre / 1¾ pint pudding basin. Prepare a steamer or half fill a large saucepan with water and bring to the boil.

Cream the butter or margarine with the sugar in a mixing bowl until light and fluffy. Beat in the eggs gradually, adding a little of the flour if the mixture begins to curdle.

Sift the flour and baking powder together and fold lightly into the creamed mixture. Add the jam or jelly, using a skewer to draw it lightly through the mixture to create a ripple effect.

Spoon the mixture into the prepared basin, cover with greased greaseproof paper and foil and secure with string.

Put the pudding in the perforated part of the steamer, or stand it on an old saucer or plate in the pan of boiling water. The water should come halfway up the sides of the basin. Cover the pan tightly and steam the pudding over gently simmering water for 1¼–1½ hours.

Leave for 3–5 minutes at room temperature to firm up, then turn out on to a serving plate. Serve with a vanilla custard.

SERVES SIX

Useful Weights and Measures

USING METRIC OR IMPERIAL MEASURES

Throughout the book, all weights and measures are given first in metric, then in imperial. For example 100 g / 4 oz, 150 ml/ ¼ pint or 15 ml / 1 tbsp.

When following any of the recipes use either metric or imperial – do not combine the two sets of measures as they are approximate equivalents, not interchangeable.

EQUIVALENT METRIC / IMPERIAL MEASURES

Weights The following chart lists some of the metric / imperial weights that are used in the recipes.

METRIC	IMPERIAL	METRIC	IMPERIAL
15 g	½ oz	375 g	13 oz
25 g	1 oz	400 g	14 oz
50 g	2 oz	425 g	15 oz
75 g	3 oz	450 g	1 lb
100 g	4 oz	575 g	1¼ lb
150 g	5 oz	675 g	1½ lb
175 g	6 oz	800 g	1¾ lb
200 g	7 oz	900 g	2 lb
225 g	8 oz	1 kg	2¼ lb
250 g	9 oz	1.4 kg	3 lb
275 g	10 oz	1.6 kg	3½ lb
300 g	11 oz	1.8 kg	4 lb
350 g	12 oz	2.25 kg	5 lb

Liquid Measures The following chart lists some metric / imperial equivalents for liquids. Millilitres (ml), litres and fluid ounces (fl oz) or pints are used throughout.

METRIC	IMPERIAL
50 ml	2 fl oz
125 ml	4 fl oz
150 ml	¼ pint
300 ml	½ pint
450 ml	¾ pint
600 ml	1 pint

Spoon Measures Both metric and imperial equivalents are given for all spoon measures, expressed as millilitres and teaspoons (tsp) or tablespoons (tbsp).

All spoon measures refer to British standard measuring spoons and the quantities given are always for level spoons.

Do not use ordinary kitchen cutlery instead of proper measuring spoons as they will hold quite different quantities.

METRIC	IMPERIAL
1.25 ml	¼ tsp
2.5 ml	½ tsp
5 ml	1 tsp
15 ml	1 tbsp

Length All linear measures are expressed in millimetres (mm), centimetres (cm) or metres (m) and inches or feet. The following list gives examples of typical conversions.

METRIC	IMPERIAL
5 mm	¼ inch
1 cm	½ inch
2.5 cm	1 inch
5 cm	2 inches
15 cm	6 inches
30 cm	12 inches (1 foot)

MICROWAVE INFORMATION

Occasional microwave hints and instructions are included for certain recipes, as appropriate. The information given is for microwave ovens rated at 650–700 watts.

The following terms have been used for the microwave settings: High, Medium, Defrost and Low. For each setting, the power input is as follows: High = 100% power, Medium = 50% power, Defrost = 30% power and Low = 20% power.

All microwave notes and timings are for guidance only: always read and follow the manufacturer's instructions for your particular appliance. Remember to avoid putting any metal in the microwave and never operate the microwave empty.

Be very careful when heating liquids in the microwave as they can 'superheat'; i.e. the liquid's surface looks still but underneath there can be boiling bubbles that explode when the container is moved.

OVEN TEMPERATURES

Whenever the oven is used, the required setting is given as three alternatives: degrees Celsius (°C), degrees Fahrenheit (°F) and gas.

The temperature settings given are for conventional ovens. If you have a fan oven, adjust the temperature according to the manufacturer's instructions.

°C	°F	GAS
110	225	¼
120	250	½
140	275	1
150	300	2
160	325	3
180	350	4
190	375	5
200	400	6
220	425	7
230	450	8
240	475	9

Index